Developing The Modern Footballer Through Futsal

Michael Skubala and Seth Burkett

Published in 2015 by Bennion Kearny Limited.

Copyright © Bennion Kearny Ltd 2015

ISBN: 978-1-909125-92-6

Published by Bennion Kearny Limited
6 Woodside
Churnet View Road
Oakamoor
Staffordshire
ST10 3AE

www.BennionKearny.com

Inside photos courtesy of Matt Withers | www.matthewwithersphotography.com

For the rock in my life, Samantha, our little princess Gracie Rose, and the rest of my family, for all your love and support.

Michael

For all of those who continue to inspire me in everything I do.

Seth

About the Authors

Michael Skubala is the England Futsal Assistant Head Coach, a position he has held for the last five years. Prior to this, he captained the side, and holds the record number of playing appearances for England. In addition to this, Michael is the Head Coach to the England under-23 squad, Great Britain Universities, the International Futsal Academy [www.internationalfutsalacademy.com], and Loughborough University. He is currently coaching the FA Futsal Level One and Level Two awards, one of only two coaches qualified to do so. In football, Michael holds his UEFA A Licence and is Performance Manager of Loughborough University Football Club. Previously he has been assistant football coach of Great Britain Universities. On Twitter, he is @mskubala.

Seth Burkett is the last Englishman to play professional football in Brazil. In Brazil, he became aware of futsal, understanding how it was used to develop Brazilian footballers. Upon returning to England, he began to play the sport. Seth has an honours degree in Sports Science from Loughborough, as well as a Master's degree in English. His previous books include *Hobby* and *The Boy in Brazil*, declared by the Daily Mirror as 'a captivating tale of a lad who refused to give up on his dream'. On Twitter, he is @burkett86.

Acknowledgements

When Michael approached me to ask whether I wanted to help produce a book on futsal, it didn't require much thought on my behalf. 'Skubes' has had a great influence on my own development in futsal, and his approach is both innovative and engaging. I believed he had a whole host of ideas waiting to be released that could truly benefit the wider community.

Skubes is just one of a number of excellent coaches I have been fortunate enough to work with. Alongside figures such as Idafe Perez Jimenez, he is helping to shape the sport of futsal in this country. I am indebted to all of those coaches who helped shape me as a young footballer, in addition to those in Brazil who introduced me to the concept of futsal as a development tool for football.

Thanks also go to my publisher, James Lumsden-Cook, for believing in this book and helping us to develop it. The guidance of Ian Ridley has also been pivotal in developing my own writing style over the years. It was Ian who encouraged me to write as often as possible.

Skubes and I couldn't have done this without help. The contributions of England futsal goalkeeping coach Tony Elliott and England futsal sports scientist Daniel Berdejo del-Fresno – for chapters 5 and 6 – were immense. Their knowledge proved to be priceless.

Finally, thanks go to my family who continue to support me in whatever I pursue. I am truly grateful.

Seth

This book and indeed my career to date would not exist without some significant events and having so many significant people invest a great deal of time into my development, to which I am eternally grateful. First of all I would like to thank my mum, dad and family for always being there for me and supporting me in whatever I have done: playing, coaching or life.

I would also like to thank Graeme Dell for introducing me to the game of Futsal many years ago as a player, and then for opening my eyes to the coaching world. Playing under Graeme taught me many things around detail and organisation in elite performance environments. I would also like to thank my good friend and great coach James Ellis, who saw something in me as a budding young coach and gave me the opportunity to work at Loughborough University. Being in such a prestigious sporting environment has given me a number of great experiences.

James challenged me on what elite performance actually looks like, and working so closely with him on Great Britain's university football team was an incredible experience that was priceless in my personal development.

Lastly, I would like to thank Pete Sturgess, not only for believing in me and giving me the opportunity at a very early age to become an international coach, but also for being my mentor and good friend. I have been privileged to learn and work alongside a great man for many years: the conversations around coaching, coach education and performance are priceless for me to lay down my own path and style within the coaching world. Everyone you meet shapes who you are and, for me, these three people are key to where I am today in my coaching career.

Most importantly I would like to thank my beautiful wife Samantha for always being there for me and allowing me to follow my dreams. You are my rock and my world. Thank you for being there and giving birth to our amazing princess Gracie Rose. Sam you are an amazing wife and an amazing mother – this book is for you!

Michael

Illustrations (download)

If you are reading an electronic version of this book, you may find some of the illustrations difficult to explore fully on your Kindle or Nook or iPhone. Likewise, if you are reading the print version of the book and would like to get your hands on the illustrations anyway – we can help.

All the illustrations in this book are available as a freely downloadable PDF.

Download the file from the publisher's web page at: www.bennionkearny.com/Futsal.pdf

Foreword

In English football, there is a sense that we are missing players with true craft and skill. Questions are raised about the lack of English players who are capable of beating an opponent with world class dribbling skills, or who have the creativity to frighten defenders. There are few, if any, English players who can rival the quality of players like Lionel Messi, Cristiano Ronaldo, or Ronaldinho in the game. The reason appears to be that our youngsters are not practising the right kinds of skills to become top players in football.

In the past, young children would develop their physical, technical and social skills outside. They would play with their friends and spend endless hours being active; hours building up and developing their potential. Many coaches and ex-professionals in England argue for the return of 'street soccer', where kids play in the streets or the parks on their own. It is here, they argue, where they develop their skills, hone their moves, and become better players. In the street, in unorganised games, there is more contact time on the ball and the opportunity to be more expressive. However, due to modern living, English football is struggling to provide this environment for its young players and this is why futsal is so important.

The best footballers in the world, Messi and Ronaldo, recognise how futsal has contributed to making them the well-rounded players they are today. As Messi, for example, said, "As a little boy in Argentina, I played futsal on the streets and for my club. It was tremendous fun, and it really helped me become who I am."

The game is growing worldwide which is unsurprising given its positive influence on football. More countries than ever are playing the sport, with FIFA describing it as, "The fastest growing indoor sport in the world."

Spain have become one of the world's best developers of talent, in part because of their culture of futsal. Their present-day 'technical excellence' and clear technical mastery of the ball are not unsurprising when you consider the impact of futsal on the nation. There is a clear link between futsal and the development of world class players. Spain's all-time international top scorer, David Villa, played futsal until the age of nine, and said, *"Futsal is a bit more technical than football. I also think that because you play for a shorter amount of time, there are different physical requirements, because you need to run constantly."* In Spain, futsal has become *the* environment for young players to develop and polish their skills.

Futsal helps to develop creativity in players perhaps more than any other version of small-sided football. By its nature, it promotes imagination, inventiveness and skill, and also improves decision making and spatial awareness. It promotes players to learn and cope in tight spaces under pressure… a significant issue which many English players struggle with.

Now it would be unfair to blame English players for technical shortcomings. It is not their fault. They are simply the products of the environments they have been developed in. Because of the style of coaching and the landscape afforded to many young players, practice conditions have come about that focus on direct play. Basically, these practice environments have stimulated the skills of long passing and neglected players' abilities to master short passing, 1v1 situations, and handling the ball under pressure.

Therefore, if we, as a nation, wish to compete with the world's best then we need to embrace futsal as a key development tool.

I hope you find this book of value. The growth, appreciation, and mastery of coaching and playing futsal is paramount to the improvements we seek in our players' skill levels. As coaches of young players we must embrace futsal more and use it to enhance the skills and mastery of our future footballers!

Matthew Whitehouse

Football Coach, Blogger, and Author of the books - *The Way Forward: Solutions to England's Football Failings* and *Universality | The Blueprint for Soccer's New Era: How Germany and Pep Guardiola are showing us the Future Football Game*

Table of Contents

Introduction

In 1930s South America there was a problem. The rapid urbanisation of cities such as Montevideo and Sao Paulo was turning once green land into a vast concrete jungle. Football pitches were swept up into this jungle, leaving players with fewer and fewer areas to play in. A solution was needed, and Juan Carlos Ceriani provided this. Ceriani sought to adapt football so that it was not only more accessible, but also more organised. He took the game of football indoors, and established a set of rules to create futsal. Played in YMCAs between youth teams on basketball-sized courts, the sport quickly became popular.

Whilst Ceriani was creating futsal in Uruguay, a similar game was emerging in Brazil. Played in the streets of Sao Paulo, the game proved just as popular, and soon futsal had spread to all corners of South America. The first international competition took place in 1965, with Paraguay winning the South American Cup. Brazil's dominance of the sport began the following year, in the same competition, and they achieved six consecutive South American Cup successes whilst creating innovative and effective futsal techniques, such as the toe-poke. FIFA took control of futsal in 1989, creating the first official FIFA Futsal World Cup. Of the seven World Cups to date, Brazil have won five. Though football remains the most popular spectator sport in Brazil, futsal has the highest participation levels in the country, even more so than football.

Futsal has been particularly recognised in Brazil for its ability to provide a tool for developing footballers' technique. Indeed, the sport provides a fertile breeding ground for cultivating the Brazilian ideology of football. Attributes such as flair, dribbling, and innovation are cultivated on the futsal court and then transferred onto the football field. Every academy in Brazil uses futsal regularly, with the majority of young players brought up solely on futsal until around the age of 12. With its emphasis on spontaneity, confidence on the ball, and lack of formal positions, the players' talents are allowed to thrive. Graduates of the sport include Pele, Ronaldo, Robinho, and Neymar, with Pele noting how, "Futsal was important in helping to develop my ball control, quick thinking, passing... also for dribbling, balance, concentration... futsal was very, very important, no doubt."

Futsal has been used similarly to develop footballing technique in other countries. The only other winners of the FIFA Futsal World Cup – Spain – have embraced futsal, and their recent dominance of world football (UEFA European Champions 2008, 2012; World Cup winners 2010) was produced with a football ideology that was heavily influenced by futsal. Futsal forms a large portion of training programmes in the Barcelona and Real Madrid academies, where performers learn the intricate details of short, sharp passing, and pressing as a unit on the court to aid their transition to the football pitch.

The links between football and futsal are numerous, with a correlation between futsal achievement and football achievement evident in the FIFA World Rankings. It is also telling that the top three players at the 2012 Ballon d'Or – Lionel Messi, Cristiano Ronaldo, and Andrés Iniesta – all played futsal in their youth. For Messi, the sport was, "a really fun game that helped me a great deal"; for Ronaldo, "the smaller court helped my footwork skills, the nature of the game made me feel so free when I played. If it wasn't for futsal, I would definitely not be the player I am today." For Iniesta, "everything" grew from futsal.

Given the technical benefits of futsal, this is no surprise. The smaller, weighted ball travels up to seven times quicker than a football, with the reduced bounce increasing ball contact. Indeed, players will receive the ball up to twelve times more often than in an organised football match. Considering the smaller space is the equivalent of a 37-a-side game on a traditional 11-a-side pitch, upon receiving the ball a player will have to make decisions quickly and effectively. The increase in ball contact enhances a player's chances to work on individual techniques, such as dribbling, passing, and feinting.

Despite this, futsal has only been introduced in England relatively recently. A national team was established in 2003, but it was not until 2008 that the first official national league was created. Since then, participation rates have grown steadily, with youth football teams particularly embracing the sport as a means of continuing development. Despite the growing level of participation, there remains a dearth of suitably qualified futsal coaches with a full understanding of the sport. A common mistake is to believe that futsal is the same as the traditional five-a-side football played in England, whereas in reality it offers so much more.

Across the globe, futsal is played in schools as part of the national curriculum. In Spain, futsal is even played *instead* of football in schools. Although the vast majority of schools in the United Kingdom have the facilities to play futsal, they continue to prioritise other sports. These facilities also provide football teams with a place to play. This has become important more recently, as local leagues have set up winter futsal leagues in order to continue football development over a period when many football games are postponed due to bad weather. A more radical approach, where a football winter break is introduced for all youth teams to concentrate solely on futsal, could be beneficial. This would also ensure that pitches are not damaged in the harsh winter period, guaranteeing better playing surfaces later in the football season and improving football development further. Despite this, the Football Association remains reluctant to fully support futsal, with funding virtually non-existent in comparison to the 11-a-side game.

This book aims to introduce concepts and ideas that help to accelerate football development through futsal. Drills and techniques are provided to empower the learner, offering guidance for fostering spontaneity, creativity and confidence. Learning outcomes will be related to football development throughout. What should be considered across the entirety of this book is that futsal should primarily be about *having fun*, and that it should be coached in such a way to ensure enjoyment for all.

Chapter 1: The Laws of the Game

Juan Carlos Ceriani first codified the sport of futsal in the 1930s. Although he intended to replicate the game of football in a more condensed indoor space, Ceriani drew inspiration from sports as diverse as basketball, handball and water polo. When FIFA took over the running of the sport, in 1989, further rules were added, such as enabling goals to be scored with the head and specifying the exact dimensions of the ball. Futsal must now be played with a spherical ball that weighs between 400 and 440 grams, and has a circumference of not more than 64 centimetres and not less than 62 centimetres.

Largely, the basic rules of futsal mirror those of football. Both teams compete against each other, attempting to invade their opponent's territory by scoring goals whilst defending their own goal. The team who scores the most goals wins. Games last for a total of forty minutes, comprising two halves of twenty minutes. As in basketball, futsal is played with a stop-clock. This ensures that whenever the ball is not in play, the timer is stopped. The game may also be stopped for a timeout and both teams have one timeout per half. The timeout is one minute long and can be used for tactical alterations.

Each team must have five players on the court at a time. Up to nine substitutes may be used in a game, and these substitutions are not only unlimited (i.e. players can be resubstituted) but can also occur at any time, whether the ball is in play or not. A player can only be substituted if he exits the pitch in the allocated substitution zone, and his replacement must wait for this player to be off the court before he enters this game (again through the allocated substitute zone).

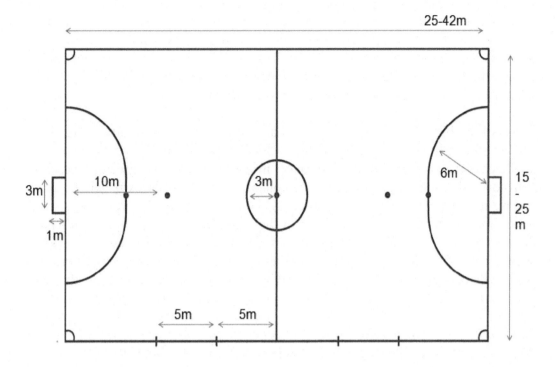

As can be seen from the image above, futsal differs from traditional five-a-side in being played to designated markings. If the ball goes off the side of the pitch or hits the ceiling then a kick-in is awarded to the relevant team to restart the play. The ball must be either on, or no further than one metre behind, the line when this kick-in is taken. Once the ball is set down, the kicker has four seconds to take the kick. Failure to take the kick within this time results in the kick-in being overturned, and given to the opposing team. Similarly, if the kicker places any part of his body on the line or inside the court whilst taking this kick, the kick gets overturned. If the ball leaves the court past the goal line then either a goal throw or corner kick is awarded. Again, these restarts must be taken within the four second time limit. This is also the case for free-kicks. For free-kicks, corner-kicks and kick-ins, defenders must be at least five metres away from the kicker.

Free-kicks are given following any action the referee deems illegal. As in basketball, any foul committed by a player counts toward an overall team foul count. Once a team has committed five fouls in a half, every foul thereafter results in a ten-metre penalty kick for the opposing team. If the foul is made inside the defender's penalty area then a six-metre penalty kick is awarded. The taker is not restricted by the four-second rule. Team fouls are wiped out at the end of each half. Punishing excessive fouling with ten-metre penalties encourages smarter defending, and also serves to protect skilful players. If a foul is deemed excessive then either a yellow or red card may be issued by the referee. If a player is sent off then his team must play with four players for two minutes or until the opposition scores a goal. Once the two minutes are up, or the opposition scores, the team may play with five once more, but the player who has been sent off must leave the court for the remainder of the game.

Players are able to move and play the ball anywhere on the court. There is no offside rule in futsal. The only player who is restricted is the goalkeeper. The goalkeeper may only touch the ball once, in his own half, in a given possession. Whenever the goalkeeper is in possession of the ball in his own half he must release it within four seconds, counted by the lead referee. Failure to do so will result in a free-kick for the opposition. If the goalkeeper is in the opponent's half, he may receive the ball as often as he wishes and is not restricted by the four-second rule. This rule has produced a tactic known as 'powerplaying' whereby a team will play with a fifth outfield player – a 'fly keeper' – leaving the goal empty. This outfield player must wear a goalkeeper's shirt with his outfield number on, and must wait until a stoppage in play to swap with the original goalkeeper. Teams may play with a fly keeper for the whole game if they wish to do so. Alternatively, the original goalkeeper can powerplay himself.

The modifications to the rules of futsal ensure that techniques can be honed and transferred successfully to the 11-a-side football field for players of all ages. As can be seen, the focus is on a dynamic game played at a quick tempo, with the unlimited substitutions allowing all players to be involved within the game.

Chapter 2: The Basics of Futsal

It is important that participants are aware of the basics of futsal. This will allow them to play the sport more effectively, getting the maximum benefits to transfer to the football pitch. As such, this chapter outlines sessions that can be implemented to introduce these basics. The basics of futsal can be split into five strands: control, passing, moving and feinting, travelling with the ball, and shooting. Each drill will relate to at least one of the strands.

Due to the smaller, heavier ball and smoother, quicker surface, different methods of control are encouraged in futsal. In football, players tend to control the ball with the instep of the foot. However, using this technique in futsal will often result in the ball bouncing too far away from the player's body. In a game where space is at a premium, a player's ball control must be excellent. To allow for this, futsal players are encouraged to use the soles of their feet to control and manipulate the ball. This enables a player to control the ball closer to their body. They can then release the ball more quickly. A player can either stop the ball dead with the sole of their foot or roll the ball in one motion to face the direction in which they wish to play. This enables the player to play quickly. The technique can also be used in football to allow a player to play quickly and is especially utilised in Spanish football, which is itself heavily influenced by futsal.

Controlling the ball with the sole of the foot also means that the ball can be passed into the player more firmly. Futsal is a quick game. As there are usually only four outfield opponents, passing the ball quickly will allow a team to open up opportunities against their opponents more easily. As discussed, the ball and surface facilitate a fast passing game. However, these factors also mean that some passes may run too fast for a teammate to run onto, either resulting in the ball going out of play or being intercepted by an opponent. To counteract this, futsal players are taught a 'scoop' pass. To perform this, a player places his foot underneath the ball and scoops it up. The subsequent bounce slows the ball down, allowing for players to time their runs better. Playing the ball in the air with a scoop pass is also an effective way of playing a pass clearly over an opponent's outstretched leg. This technique is used widely and effectively by football players influenced by futsal, an example being Lionel Messi. As in futsal, it allows for players to time their runs more efficiently whilst also breaking the lines of the opponents' defence effectively.

Once a player has made a pass, he must work towards receiving the ball once again by moving. Futsal is a game which relies on clever rotations to unlock an opponents' defence. Players have no set positions and are expected to take up positions all over the court. This mirrors the modern day football midfield, where players rotate fluidly to make space to receive and play the ball. If space is tight – which it often is in futsal – then a player may have to feint to create the space to receive the ball. The concept of feinting is vital in futsal. Within this concept, an attacker fakes to go one way, fooling the defender into following him. The attacker then turns back quickly, gaining space between himself and the defender in the process.

Although futsal is a game that relies heavily on passing and possession, there are numerous opportunities to travel with the ball in each game. These are enhanced by the counter-attacking nature of the sport. Effective counter-attacks require players to run quickly with the ball in order to utilise the space left by their opponents. Travelling with the ball is not only effective in counter-attacks, though. Dribbling past an opponent has a much greater effect than in the eleven-a-side game, as it removes at least a quarter of the opponents' defence. As there are fewer players than in football, the opportunities to isolate a defender become more frequent, meaning that the dribble can be attempted regularly. If the dribble is attempted at the wrong moment, however, it can have devastating effects, leaving the player's team open to a counter-attack. Knowing when to attempt the dribble and when to play safe is therefore very important. If a player does decide to dribble, then it is imperative that he has close control. If the ball is overrun then his team is susceptible to a counter-attack. This considered, it is no surprise that players such as Neymar and Lionel Messi attribute their close control and decision-making to their grounding in futsal.

All of these strands are vital when playing futsal to allow a team to fulfil the main objective of the sport: scoring more goals than the opposition. To do this, a team needs to have effective shooting. The size of the area in futsal means that shots can be taken from most places on the court. As with the other strands, there are some variations with the basic principles of shooting when compared to football. In futsal, shots need to be powerful. The reduced space available means that the shooter may have to get shots away quickly. In turn, this may mean that the shooter does not have enough time to perform a big enough backlift to generate sufficient power in his shot. A modification used in futsal to provide this power is the toe-poke. Traditionally (and wrongly) stereotyped as a poor technique in football, the toe-poke not only generates a powerful shot at goal but can also catch the goalkeeper by surprise. This is important, as shooting is a big risk in futsal. If a shot is tame and easy to catch for the goalkeeper, then he can quickly start a counter-attack for his own team. Shots therefore need to be powerful enough so that the goalkeeper is unable to catch the ball. Furthermore, the shooter is often encouraged to aim towards the back post. As there is no offside rule in futsal, placing an attacker at the back post will increase the options for the shooter – either shooting at goal himself or passing the ball to the attacker on the back post, eliminating the goalkeeper and providing the player with a simple tap-in. Transferred to the eleven-a-side game, these principles will improve a player's decision-making in the final third and encourage him to be more creative with his finishing, as well as teaching him the importance of finishing an action at goal. The toe-poke is an especially useful technique, and is used by numerous football players influenced by futsal – Ronaldinho's goal against Chelsea in the 2005 UEFA Champions League round of 16 being a prime example.

The following pages outline sessions that can be used to work on these strands. These sessions are split into drills, with each drill working on at least one strand. Ways to adapt the session are given, whilst the benefits for football development are also stressed.

Control

Session: Control 1 - Finding Key Areas

- **Recommended Time:** 20 minutes
- **Number of Players:** 8+

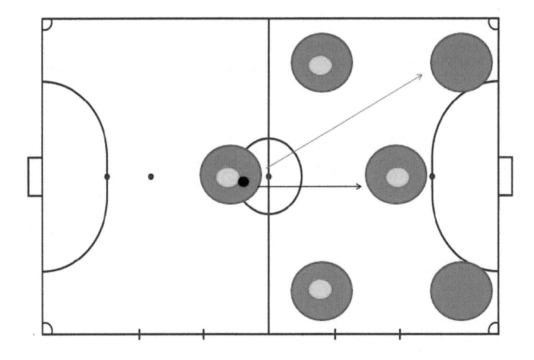

Focus of Session: Control and passing.

Objectives: To show players how to control and manipulate the ball using futsal techniques whilst understanding the important positions on the futsal court.

Organisation: Six cones are laid down to mark key areas (where opponents can best be exploited, giving the best opportunities to create goals) for players on the court. Players work in groups of four, occupying four of the six areas. Players pass the ball to a team-mate in another area or dribble to an unoccupied area before releasing the ball. Once the ball is released the player must move to an unoccupied area.

Coaching Factors:

- Encourage players to use the soles of their feet to control the ball and move it offline (around cones) as quickly as possible.
- Secure and set-up the ball in one motion ready to pass.
- Use the sole of the foot to drive away from a cone in a forwards or backwards motion.
- Use the sole of the foot to push the ball into space to initiate dribbling or running with the ball.

Progression Ideas:

- Place another set of six cones within the key areas to create contextual interference.
- Always make sure half of the key areas are occupied.
- Add a defender to intercept the ball. This defender has his own ball and attempts to intercept the ball being passed whilst dribbling his own ball around the area.

Links to Football:

- Players work on using the soles of their feet to drive the ball away from pressure. This is an excellent technique for being in tight areas in football, such as in and around zone 14 and the penalty area.
- Learning how to control to keep the ball close under high pressure situations.
- Players learn the importance of manipulating the ball quickly and moving into a new area once they have released the ball.

Session: Control 2 - College Dropout

- **Recommended Time:** 20 minutes
- **Number of Players:** 8+

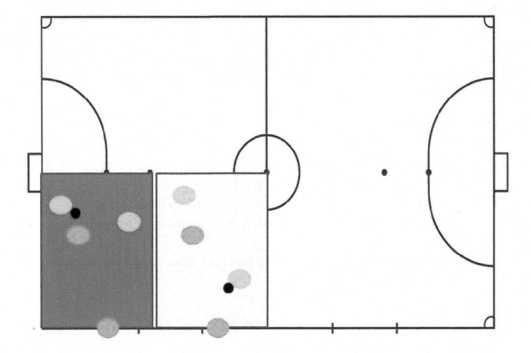

Focus of Session: Control, passing and feinting to receive the ball.

Objectives: To create high pressure situations to mirror game situations.

Organisation: Create a 5m x 10m box. In the area play a 2v2. A goal is scored by stopping the ball on the opposition's end line. Whenever a pair have the ball, one of the opposing players must drop out onto their own defensive line and can only defend the line whilst out of possession. The other player defends the two attacking players who aim to stop the ball on the end line.

Coaching Factors:

- Direction play to focus on control in tight areas and evading opponents with oriented sole control.
- Feint movement to create time and space.
- Take first touch in or out of pressure to create space for team mate.

Progression Ideas:

- Make area bigger or smaller depending on difficulty and needs of players. (NB: A messy looking game is a good learning game).
- Defender doesn't have to drop out onto back line when out of possession.
- Bounce game - 3 minute games. Whoever wins moves up a box. Losers move down a box and play other opponents.

Links to Football:

- Allows players to work in very tight areas and experiment with ways of keeping the ball facing forward.
- A good secure confident touch into pressure creates space that a team-mate can exploit as it engages defenders.
- Great for number 10s, midfield players and wingers.

Session: Control 3 - Control the Line

- **Recommended Time:** 20 minutes
- **Number of Players:** 8+

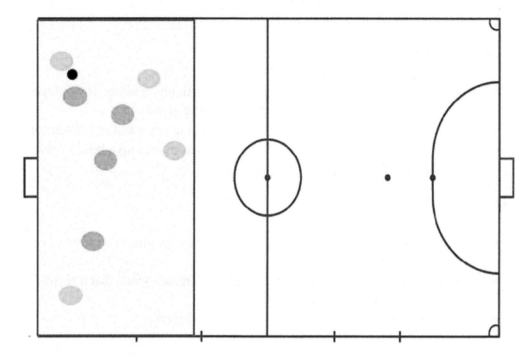

Focus of Session: Control, passing and movement.

Objectives: To understand the importance of keeping possession and having excellent control techniques whilst under pressure.

Organisation: Working across a third of the court, teams of four attempt to score by stopping the ball on the opponent's line. Goals are also awarded if the opposing team kicks a ball off the court. This encourages players to stay on the ball using different types of control under pressure.

Coaching Factors:

- Encourage different types of control.
- Stay on the ball if pressed and remain calm.
- Encourage defenders to tackle so they retain possession rather than kicking the ball out of the play.

Progression Ideas:

- A team can only score if they stop it on the line.
- Players can pass or dribble in to restart the game.
- Restrict touches to a maximum of two.

Links to Football:

- This is a high-paced possession game that doesn't reward defenders just kicking the ball out. To be successful you must retain possession. This is important in all areas of football.
- Encourages clever play when highly pressed in corners. Full backs or wingers need to make clever decisions in areas under high pressure to keep possession.
- Working in a tight area allows midfield players to interact fluidly as a unit of four.

Passing, Moving and Feinting

Session: Passing, Moving and Feinting 1 - Checkmate

- **Recommended Time:** 20 minutes
- **Number of Players:** 6+

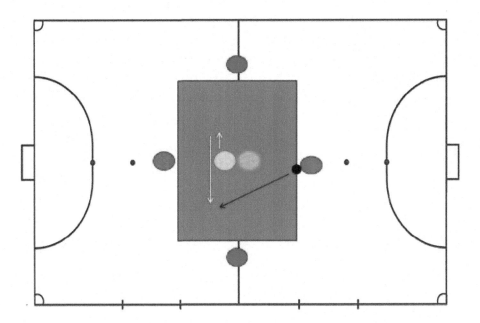

Focus of Session: Movement to receive the ball, feinting, control and passing.

Objectives: To lose your opponent in a tight area in order to receive the ball with as much time as possible.

Organisation: Four players are positioned around the perimeter of a 5 by 10

16

metre box. Inside the box are two players. These players compete against each other in a one versus one. A player must receive the ball from the outside of the box and then play a pass to another player. If the defender intercepts the ball then he gains possession.

Coaching Factors:

- Assess movement to receive the ball.
- Ensure players receive the ball under high pressure.
- Players should receive the ball on their 'safe side' if they are pressed.
- Work on the timing of a players feint – they should move two metres in one direction to gain five metres in another direction.

Progression Ideas:

- Play two versus two in the middle.
- Award a goal for every ten passes completed.

Links to Football:

- This game requires players to create space and lose defenders in tight areas. They must do so with clever body movements. As such, this game is excellent for central midfielders and strikers.
- Players must be agile and control the ball close to their body with intent to play forwards.
- Once a pass is made, a player must immediately look to receive the ball again.

Session: Passing, Moving and Feinting 2 - Lose your Man

- **Recommended Time:** 20 minutes
- **Number of Players:** 8+

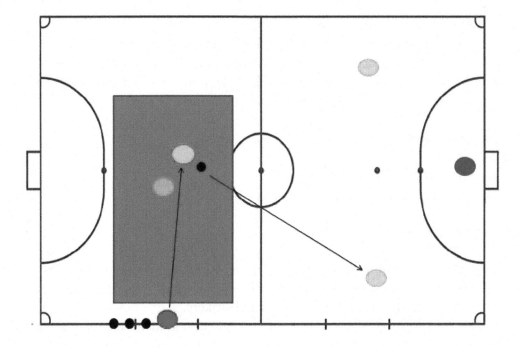

Focus of Session: Movement to receive the ball, feinting, control and passing.

Objectives: For a player to feint and lose their opponent, giving them space to receive the ball, play forwards and attempt to score.

Organisation: A player sets up on the outside of the area with the balls. He plays a ball into a player in the central zone. This player is playing against a defender and must create the space to receive the ball. Once he receives the ball he must play forwards to one of the two pivots. The pivot then sets him for a shot at goal. The other pivot gets on the back post for the player's shot.

Coaching Factors:

- Work on the timing and movement of the feint.
- The player feinting should move past the shoulder of the defender in order to affect him.
- The attacker should close his hips to engage the defender.
- Find space to play forward quickly.
- Combine with the pivot players to produce an end product.

Progression Ideas:

- Play both ways with two games going on at the same time to add interference.
- Make it a 2v2 in the box rather than 1v1.

Links to Football:

- Midfielders need to work in tight areas to lose defenders.
- Wingers need to run off the ball and in behind defenders.
- Players need to feint to receive the ball in tight areas.

Session: Passing, Moving and Feinting 3 - Endzone

- **Recommended Time:** 20 minutes
- **Number of Players:** 8+

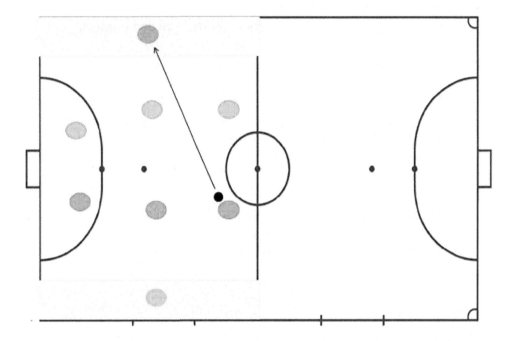

Focus of Session: Movement to receive the ball, feinting, control and passing.

Objectives: To keep possession and play forward into a fixed pivot when the opportunity arises.

Organisation: The game is played lengthways across a full-size court. Zones are marked out for the pivots at either end, which are five metres long and run for the width of the area. These areas are occupied only by the pivots, and players from the middle cannot enter. In the middle of the area there is a 3v3 possession game. To score a goal, these players in the middle must play a pass to their pivot.

Coaching Factors:

- Players should attempt to play forwards whenever possible.
- Players should position their body so that they can receive the ball to play forward.
- Play with as few touches as possible.
- Ensure the pivots in the endzones work laterally to create passing lines and options.
- Clever, imaginative play and innovation in order to keep the ball or play forward should be encouraged.

Progression Ideas:

- Once the ball goes to the pivot, the team that played the ball in receives the ball back off the same pivot and attacks the other way.
- Once a player passes into the pivot he becomes the pivot and the pivot rotates into the middle area.
- Place a defender in the zone to screen off the pivot.

Links to Football:

- Players have to play forward to a pivot/striker as quickly as possible.
- This requires creative passing combinations in high areas, such as zone 14.
- A false number 9 needs to be able to rotate back into midfield. A pivot needs to be able to rotate with his teammates.
- Forward players need to move cleverly to lose their markers and receive the ball.

Travelling with the Ball

Session: Travelling with the Ball 1 - Fightball

- **Recommended Time:** 20 minutes
- **Number of Players:** 8+

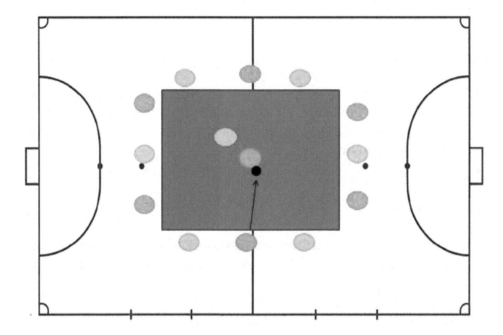

Focus of Session: Travelling with the ball, control and movement.

Objectives: To attempt to stay on the ball for as long as possible.

Organisation: A 10x10 metre box is created in the middle of the court. Players position themselves evenly around the box. Inside the box a 1v1 is played. The game is initiated by a player from the outside playing a pass to the attacker in the box. This attacker protects the ball from the defender in the box, moving around with the ball if possible. Once the attacker feels uncomfortable he plays the ball back to a player on the outside of the box. This player then takes over as the attacker, and another player from outside the box will switch with the defender. If the defender wins possession from the attacker then he becomes the attacker. The coach times how long each player is able to hold onto the ball.

Coaching Factors:

- Use the sole to secure the ball.
- The sole of the foot can also be used to move the ball whilst travelling under pressure.
- Understand when to travel and when to protect.
- Use the body to protect the ball.
- Create a barrier from the defender by protecting the ball sideways on.

Progression Ideas:

- If a player holds onto the ball for 1 minute then he can break out from the area and shoot at goal.
- Turn the session into a competition. If a player gets tackled then he is out. The winner is the last one who remains in the box.

Links to Football:

- Use of the sole of the foot for close control is important in tight areas.
- Close control and staying on the ball whilst travelling is important for players in all positions.
- Players are encouraged not to panic and give away possession.
- Travelling with the ball in tight areas mirrors wingers travelling into close pressurised areas such as the penalty area.

Session: Travelling with the Ball 2 - Braveheart

- **Recommended Time:** 20 minutes
- **Number of Players:** 8+

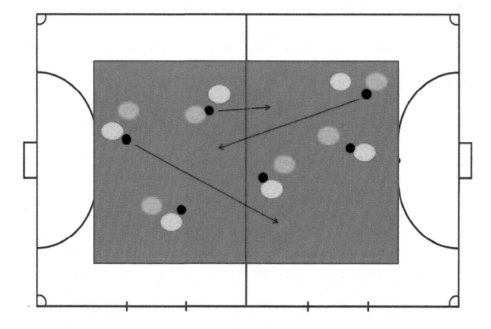

Focus of Session: Travelling with the ball, control and defending.

Objectives: To avoid opponents by travelling with the ball.

Organisation: A 15x15 metre area with a marked halfway line is created. Players pair up and play against each other in a 1v1. Up to 20 players can play their 1v1 games in the area at the same time. To score a goal, a player must dribble past his opponent – avoiding players from the other games going on at the same time – and cross the halfway line. Once he has done this, he has to attempt to come back over the halfway line to score again.

Coaching Factors:

- Can players use the sole of their foot to evade their opponent whilst travelling over the line?
- When travelling, players should keep the ball as close to their body as possible.
- Work on when to run with the ball and when to dribble.

Progression Ideas:

- Adapt the size of the area to increase or decrease the challenge accordingly.
- Use the extra players in the area to bounce passes to gain more points.

Links to Football:

- This game works on ball mastery with contextual interference.
- Players must be comfortable when isolated in possession in tight areas.
- Wingers must beat opponents in tight areas to gain territory.

Session: Travelling with the Ball 3 - Need for Speed

- **Recommended Time:** 20 minutes
- **Number of Players:** 8+

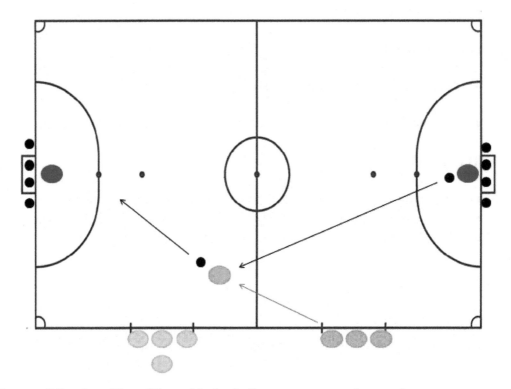

Focus of Session: Travelling with the ball, movement and control.

Objectives: To counter-attack the opposition's goal by travelling with the ball as quickly as possible.

Organisation: This game is played on a full court. Teams of four outfield players line up in their substitution gate at the side of the pitch. Each team has a goalkeeper. The game is begun by a goalkeeper throwing the ball to the first player in his line. This player attacks the opposition goal unopposed. As soon as this attack is over, the opposition goalkeeper throws the ball to the first player in his team's line, who must counter-attack quickly by travelling with the ball. The player who previously attacked now defends. Once this counter-attack is completed, the original goalkeeper initiates another counter-attack by throwing to his teammate to create a 2v1. This teammate is encouraged to travel with the ball himself to score a goal. This pattern is repeated, with the game becoming a 2v2,

26

then a 3v2, 3v3, 4v3, 4v4. Once all players have attacked the game is reset.

Coaching Factors:

- Travel as quickly as possible to score a goal on the counter-attack.
- As the game progresses, decision-making becomes a greater factor. Players need to understand when to travel, when to pass, and when to shoot.
- Players should attempt to end an attack to slow the counter-attack of their own attack.
- Be positive on the ball.

Progression Ideas:

- Limit the players involved in the game to a maximum of three. This will create more space, therefore giving greater opportunities to travel with the ball.
- Instead of stopping the game once everyone has attacked, the rules can be altered. If a player loses possession then he must drop out of the game. Eventually the game should go back down to 1v1.

Links to Football:

- Counter-attacks must be executed quickly in both futsal and football.
- Speed and effective decision-making are imperative.
- Players must travel with the ball at speed in tight areas.
- Players must also run with the ball when in greater space to cover ground and gain an end product.

Shooting

Session: Shooting 1 - Get Set to Shoot

- **Recommended Time:** 20 minutes
- **Number of Players:** 8+

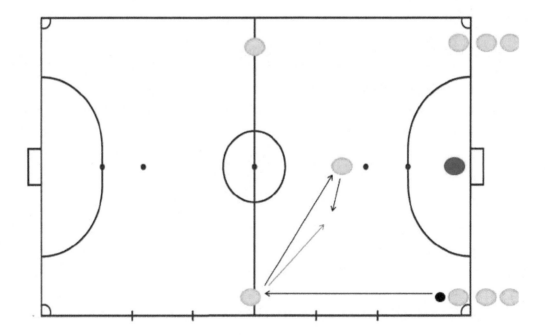

Focus of Session: Shooting, movement and passing.

Objectives: To shoot first time from a set back from a pivot.

Organisation: Working on half a court, players evenly distribute themselves between the two corners on the touchline. One player is a pivot and he works in the middle of the court. Two players – shooters – position themselves on the halfway line, one opposite each group of players. The practice starts by the group on the far side playing a pass down the line to their delegated shooter. This player receives the ball and plays a pass into the pivot, who sets the ball back for a first time shot. Each player follows their pass, so the passer becomes the shooter, the shooter becomes the pivot, and the pivot joins the back of the opposite line of passers. Once this is done, the group on the near side get their shot off, and the two groups continue to alternate throughout the practice.

Coaching Factors:

- Shooters should try to 'finish the action' by striking the ball with power.
- Aim high with shots. This, coupled with striking the ball with power, will make it harder for the shot to be caught and the opposition to counter-attack.
- Use different techniques to strike the ball: striking with the laces, the instep, and toe-poking the ball are all good ways to finish.
- The pivot should use the sole of his foot to set the ball for the shooter.

Progression Ideas:

- Add in a player to defend against the pivot.
- Once the pivot has set the ball back he then attempts to get on the back post to give the shooter a second option.
- Put two players in to defend against both the pivot and the shooter.

Links to Football:

- Football requires players to finish in a number of different ways.
- In tight areas players do not have the time to generate power in their shots with a big back-lift. Striking the ball with a toe-poke enables the shooter to generate power in his shot without the use of a back-lift and also prevents the goalkeeper from getting set.
- Practising finishing in a smaller goal makes accuracy more important.
- As futsal balls are harder than footballs, regular practice over a long period of time will increase shot power.

Session: Shooting 2 - Special Delivery

- **Recommended Time:** 20 minutes
- **Number of Players:** 8+

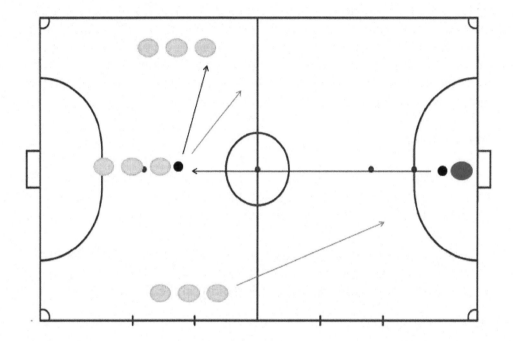

Focus of Session: Shooting, movement and passing.

Objectives: To create finishing opportunities – focusing on finishing at the far post – when attacking with an overload.

Organisation: Players are split into three groups on the halfway line – one group in the centre, one on the left and one on the right. The goalkeeper begins the practice by throwing the ball to the central player. The central player then passes the ball to one of the outside groups. He then becomes the defender in a 2v1, with the two wide players becoming the attackers. Once these two have attacked, they become defenders. The goalkeeper throws the ball to the central player once again, and all three players attack the two defenders to make a 3v2. Once this attack is over the practice is reset.

30

Coaching Factors:

- Work on the correct technique for different finishes.
- Attacks should be quick.
- Support runs should be timed to open up specific passing lines.
- As there are no offsides, players can break the line of the defence.
- One attacker should position himself on the back post. The shooter needs to be aware of any presence at the back post when he takes his shot. This presence should also move the goalkeeper away from their near post.
- Attacks must be finished to avoid being counter-attacked.

Progression Ideas:

- Introduce a time limit for attackers to get their shot off.
- Add in gates over the halfway line. If the defenders win the ball back then they can score a goal by running with the ball through the gate.

Links to Football:

- Different types of finishes are required for different areas and situations in football.
- This practice improves decision-making in front of goal – when to shoot, when to pass and when to travel with the ball.
- Shots must be 'finished' to prevent counter-attacks.
- Attackers need to break the line of defence with passes.
- They also need to make clever runs to support attacks.

Session: Shooting 3 - Stick or Twist

- **Recommended Time:** 20 minutes
- **Number of Players:** 8+

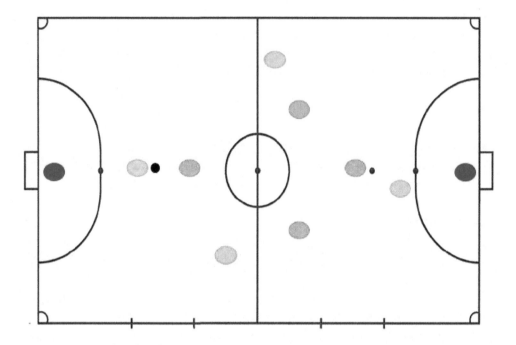

Focus of Session: Shooting, passing and movement.

Objectives: This is a practice which rewards risk-taking with finishing.

Organisation: Two evenly matched teams play a normal game across a full court until a goal is scored. Once the goal is scored, the team can decide to either 'stick' or 'twist'. If they stick, then it counts as a normal goal. If the team twists, however, and they score again then this goal is worth two. Should the team decide to twist again then their next goal will be worth four. This doubling continues until the team decides to 'stick' or the opposition score. If the opposition scores then all goals which have not been twisted are disregarded.

Coaching Factors:

- Use the correct technique to execute different finishes.
- Know when to risk and when to keep (relates to possession, shots, and sticking/twisting).
- 'Finish the attack' to prevent counter-attacks.

Progression Ideas:

- When a team scores they get a condition for their next goal (i.e. must be a first-time finish)
- If working on a certain type of finish then all goals scored with this type of finish can be awarded as double, i.e. toe-poke finishes are worth two goals.

Links to Football:

- This is a shooting and finishing game played under pressure.
- Decision-making when under pressure is vital – especially if 1-0 down. This game assesses how players react in such a situation.
- Shots must be 'finished' to prevent counter-attacks.
- Players need to understand when to bank and when to stick. This relates to a number of different concepts in football, such as possession and shooting.

Chapter 3: Defending

As with modern football, futsal is a sport which requires all members of a team to defend together as a unit. In both sports, teams have to deny the opposition territorial advantage. To do this, players need to co-operate, read the game well, be strong in 1v1 situations, position their bodies to force opponents into particular areas on the pitch, and cut off passing options.

Broadly speaking, there are two methods of defending in football: as a deep, organised defensive unit, and pressing high up the pitch. This chapter introduces three concepts of defending in futsal which can be used to improve an individual or a team's defensive capabilities. Sessions are given to work on a zonal diamond, a high press, and a man-to-man system of defending.

The zonal diamond incorporates three lines of defence. In a set-up of 1-1-2-1, a pivot (top man) plays at the top of the diamond, two wingers play slightly deeper than him, and at the back is the *cierre* (back man). The defenders stay in their zonal areas and do not follow the attackers; instead, they take their own positions on court from the position of the ball. The emphasis in this system of defending is on absorbing pressure and cutting out passing options for the opposition, particularly into the middle of the court. The aim is to eventually force the opponents into an area – usually wide – where the defending team can win the ball and counter-attack swiftly.

The principles of defending in a zonal diamond are the same as for those teams who defend deep to play on the counter-attack in football. Once a team is organised in their defensive system, however, they are able to press. In both futsal and football, teams should press on triggers. Triggers are stimuli which show defenders that their opponent is uncomfortable on the ball and struggling to retain possession. Examples may be a slow, inaccurate pass, a bad first touch, a negative touch, or a pass into an area with a defensive overload, to name a few. Defenders need to be able to recognise these triggers and press aggressively from them. The more uncomfortable a player is in possession, the more aggressively they should be pressed. In this instance, aggressive pressure refers to the defender getting within a yard of their opponent, applying physical pressure and attacking the front of their hips (as this is where the ball will be). Teams may transition from a zonal diamond to a full press upon a trigger.

Alternatively, teams may decide to press from the beginning of a play. In the high press there are also three lines of defence, though the formation alters to a 1-1-1-2 with the top two players starting much higher up the court when pressing. When

34

defending in this system it is imperative that players press 'cleverly'. Running at a high intensity alone will not allow a defender to press cleverly. Instead, he must position his body, time his approach, and work off his team-mates to press effectively. These exercises stress this by pointing out factors such as pressing an opponent onto his weak foot. This should make him more uncomfortable and increase the chances of regaining possession. The supporting defenders then take their own position off the level of pressure on the ball. If the pressure is not aggressive then they need to have a greater emphasis on covering passing lines to limit an opponent's passing options. If the pressure is aggressive, however, then they can get tighter to their own man. This concept is similar to the man-to-man defending style, which the last of the three sessions in this chapter works on.

Again, defending man-to-man has the same broad principles as defending in football: being aware of where both the ball and the man are at all times and shutting down quickly and effectively. Practising these sessions in a futsal environment has great benefits for football development. The tighter areas and faster speed of the ball require players to make decisions quicker and more regularly, with poor decisions often being punished emphatically.

These sessions must be played out at match intensity in order to gain the maximum benefits for football development. Attackers should be managed so that they move the ball quickly to test defenders, and the defending team should be coached so that they work together effectively to defend as a unit in each defensive system. These systems are not rigid. Indeed, due to the dynamic nature of futsal there are many transitions. As such, these systems provide fluid concepts which change depending upon the situation.

Session: Defending as a Zonal Diamond 1

- **Recommended Time:** 20 mins
- **Number of Players:** 9+

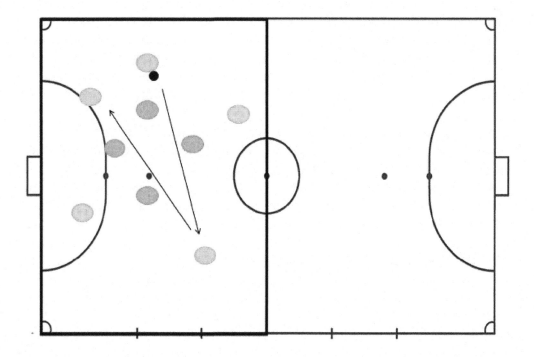

Focus of Session: Movement and working as a unit.

Objectives: To understand the basics of defending in a zonal diamond.

Organisation: Play in a square of 20x20m (can be played across half a court). Four defenders work together to attempt to win the ball back from an overload of attackers (5+). The attackers score goals by playing passes in between, or through, the defensive players. To prevent this from happening, the four defenders must defend in a tight diamond shape.

Coaching Factors:

- Defenders must understand that wherever the ball is, the first defender is the top of the diamond.
- The next two players are the wingers. They protect the middle of the diamond and stop passes coming through.
- The player furthest away from the ball is the back man. He screens the ball through the diamond and communicates to the other three players.
- The defending team should always be in a diamond shape in relation to the ball. The distances between players will depend on the defensive pressure on the ball.
- When defending, the role of the top man is to force the ball down one side to half the court. This makes the attacker's area smaller to play in.
- Wingers must press the ball in wide areas and cover when the ball is on the other side.
- The role of the back man is to screen the play and be the last line of defence.

Progression Ideas:

- Defenders score points by regaining possession within a certain number of passes by the attacking team, i.e. within ten passes.
- If the defenders get played through they lose a goal.

Links to Football:

- The game of football is played in diamonds. This can be used as a defensive exercise for a midfield four or a midfield playing with a lone striker.
- Preventing passes being made through a defensive unit forces opponents to play in wider, more isolated areas of play for longer, increasing the chances of regaining possession.
- This exercise encourages defenders to shut off passing lines and can be adapted to work on pressing as a unit. Both are key factors in football.
- Alternatively, the attackers, who are playing with an overload, need to have patience during possession. This mirrors a team playing against an opponent who has had a player sent off.

Session: Defending as a Zonal Diamond 2

- **Recommended Time:** 20 minutes
- **Number of Players:** 9+

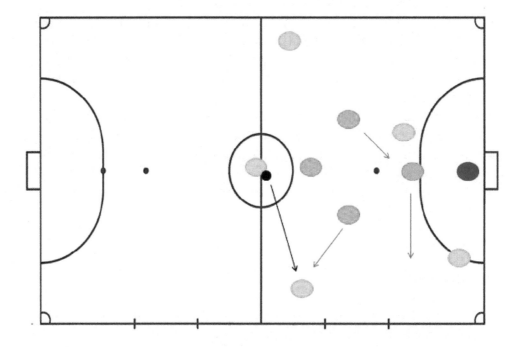

Focus of Session: Movement, working as a unit and transitions.

Objectives: To understand the principles of defending in a zonal diamond and how the shape of this diamond will change in different contexts.

Organisation: Five attackers play against four defenders. These defenders must play zonally as they cannot match themselves up man-to-man. The goalkeeper begins the practice by throwing the ball to the attacking team who try to score. The defending team work on their diamond shape at all times. If they win the ball they can counter to score.

Coaching Factors:

- All decisions in the diamond should be made in relation to the pressure on the ball.
- When the ball is in central areas the team must prevent passes being played through the middle of their diamond.
- If the ball is in the team's defensive half they must get pressure on the ball. The top man's role is to try and win the ball. However, he must be patient in attempting to do this. If he cannot then he should show the ball to the wide areas. The winger's job is to protect the pass into top players. The back man and goalkeeper will communicate to them to help them press certain lines. The back man's job is to screen a top player (preferably in front) to stop passing lines into the opposition's most advanced player.
- When the ball travels to wide areas the top of the diamond becomes the winger and the shape moves. This concept is known as box-diamond-box, which also describes the transition. The winger presses the ball aggressively and the top player tries to cut off passes across the full width of the court. The opposite winger moves himself inside to half the court and acts as protection against the opposition's top man. The back man moves out wide to cover the first winger.

Progression Ideas:

- Mark out the areas where the defence should show the attacking team into, in order to win the ball back, i.e. in the wide areas.
- Work on defenders pressing their opponents onto their weaker feet. This is advanced level defending and should improve the chances of regaining possession of the ball.

Links to Football:

- The 1-1-2-1 shape is crucial in all areas of the 11-a-side game. You can draw diamonds within, or between, units in all aspects of football.
- Each unit needs to be compact so they cannot be played through.
- Modern defending in football requires all players to defend, with the forwards acting as the first line of defence. All members of the team interact to defend as one overall unit.
- Players need to understand when, and how, to press in relation to the ball and other players.
- Forcing a team to play into a certain area increases the chances of

regaining possession. Pushing an opponent away from goal also reduces the chance of them producing an end product.

- Players will often have to defend against an attacking overload. Full backs may overlap, an opponent may have a numerical advantage in midfield, and teams will often counter-attack at pace. Teams need to cope with these overloads by forcing the play into certain areas.

Session: Defending as a Zonal Diamond 3 (Advancing to Press)

- **Recommended Time:** 20 minutes
- **Number of Players:** 10-18

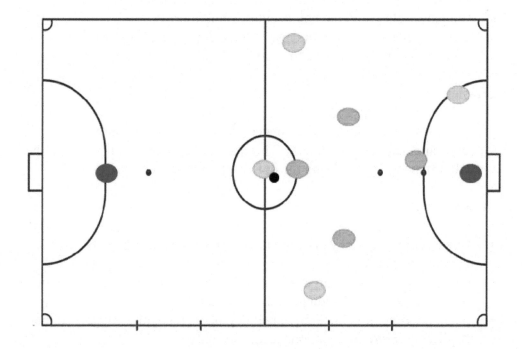

Focus of Session: Movement, working as a unit, pressing and transitions.

Objectives: To transition from a defensive diamond shape to a more pressured form of defence, such as a 1-1-3 (kite) formation.

Organisation: Set up as a normal 5v5 game on a full court. Both teams must drop off into a defensive diamond if they lose possession. Once stable in their diamond, a team may advance and begin to press their opponents.

Coaching Factors:

- Recover quickly into the diamond shape upon losing possession.
- Players should press and try and win the ball back on triggers. Triggers indicate that a team is uncomfortable in possession and that the ball can

41

be regained. They include the following: slow play, a negative pass, a bad first touch, and when the opposition is disorganised. At first a coach may verbally aid the defenders so that they can recognise triggers.

- Defenders should be encouraged to win the ball in wide areas whenever possible.
- Defenders should cut off passing options.
- The defensive diamond should never be played through.
- The player closest to the ball decides when to press.
- Once this player presses, the rest of the team must act accordingly. Usually they will also have to press.

Progression Ideas:

- Play with three teams. If you concede then you must leave the pitch.
- Limit attackers to two touches. This should encourage them to move the ball around quicker, testing the defence more thoroughly.

Links to Football:

- This is a great way to work on elite and developing footballers' recognition of triggers.
- As a futsal ball travels up to seven times quicker it is harder to spot and execute an action depending on those triggers.
- When pressing, it is imperative that defenders recognise triggers so that they can pressure their opponents accordingly.
- This exercise also works on pressing as a unit. Once one player presses, the rest must also press. This makes it harder for an opponent to retain possession.
- When a player goes back to playing football, the play will be slower, therefore making it easier to read triggers.
- Recognising and acting upon triggers is vital when counter-pressing. This is a system which relies on swift counter-attacks upon regaining the ball. To regain the ball the whole team presses collectively, pressing aggressively on triggers.
- Often in football, the striker presses the goalkeeper. If his teammates do not press with him, the opponents are able to pass their way out of the pressure and attack with a one-man advantage. If players understand the importance of pressing as a unit, it makes it harder for the opponents to retain possession.

Session: Defending in a High Press 1 (1-1-1-2)

- **Recommended Time:** 20 minutes
- **Number of Players:** 12

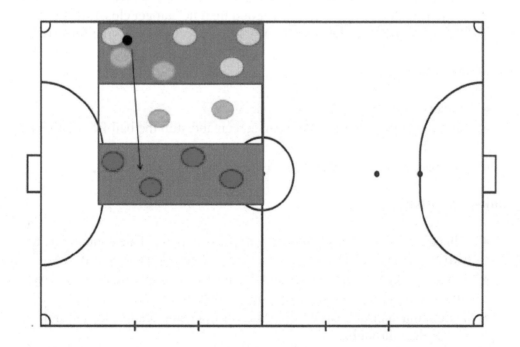

Focus of Session: Movement, working as a unit and transitions.

Objectives: To prevent the ball from being passed forwards whilst defending

43

outnumbered. This mirrors a 1-1-1-2 system of pressing.

Organisation: Three grids of about 10x15m are set out. Players are split into three teams of four with each team occupying one of the grids. The team in the central grid start off as defenders. The defensive team attempt to win the ball back but can send only two players into the attackers' grid. The attackers must transfer the ball over to the opposite side as soon as they can. If the defenders regain possession then they switch with the team that lost the ball, who now become defenders. Kicking the ball out of play does not count as regaining possession.

Coaching Factors:

- The defender closest to the ball tries to apply as much pressure as possible.
- The second defender should either cover the first defender to prevent the forward pass or press the passing line. This second option is more of a risk as it leaves space behind the defenders.
- The second defender must take his position from the pressure on the ball. If the first defender's pressure is good then he can get closer; if it is not then cover needs to be applied to stop the opposition playing forward.

Progression Ideas:

- Players must play 3v2 in each zone.
- Resting players in the middle can screen and stop the ball from going through.
- The ball must be played through the areas on the floor.

Links to Football:

- This exercise teaches players how to press in pairs. This could relate to two strikers working together or a central midfield partnership.
- It also teaches when to cover and when you can apply more secondary and tertiary pressure, depending on the pressure on the ball.
- Defending central areas as a pair makes opposing teams play around rather than through.

Session: Defending in a High Press 2 (1-1-1-2)

- **Recommended Time:** 20 minutes
- **Number of Players:** 11

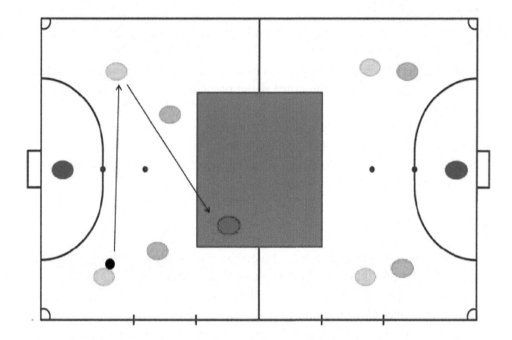

Focus of Session: Movement, working as a unit and pressing.

Objectives: For the first line of defence to learn the importance of altering their body shape to prevent the ball being played through central areas.

Organisation: Two teams of four play across a full court with a goalkeeper in each goal. One of these teams is attacking and the other defending. They must defend in a 1-1-2 formation, with the attackers playing in a 2-2. Two players from each team play in the opposition half and two play in their own half. They must not go in to the other half. In the centre of the court a 10x10m box is created and filled by an unopposed floating player.

The practice is begun by the goalkeeper throwing the ball out to one of the two closest attackers. The attacking team then attempts to play the ball into the floating player in the central box. If he receives the ball then he can turn and play

45

into the two forward players who attempt to score. The front two defenders must prevent the ball from being played into the central area.

Coaching Factors:

- The first defender out to the ball must get their body shape right to protect the middle of the court.
- They must not exaggerate their body position so much that they are dribbled past by the attacker.
- The second defending player has to cover this defender, making sure he protects the middle of the court if the pressure on the ball is not good enough.
- All defenders should be on their front foot.
- Body shape should go from initially being big, flat, and wide to stop players from playing forward, to sideways on and aggressive once closer to the ball to make play predictable.

Progression Ideas:

- Once an attacking player has played the ball into the floating player in the middle, he can then join in with the attack to make it a 3v2 overload.
- As soon as the floating player has his first touch in the middle area, a defender may enter the box to press him.
- Have a defender against the floating player to make it an opposed situation.
- Once the ball is played into the middle, a normal game begins, with players allowed anywhere on court. The floating player steps out of the practice and is not involved.
- Play in both directions so that both teams have to practise defending effectively in high areas.
- Play a normal game where players must play into the box before their team scores.
- Change the size of the box.

Links to Football:

- Teams no longer rely solely on their defenders to defend. In modern day football a team must defend together, with the first line of defence coming from the forward players. This exercise allows players to understand the importance of the first line of defence pressing and the impact that can have on a team if it is not done well enough.

- Pressing has to be clever. Defenders cannot just run quickly to the ball and expect to press effectively. Players must support each other, press aggressively on triggers, and alter their body shapes accordingly.
- Making play predictable and forcing opponents wide as a unit stops threatening passes through lines of defence.
- This exercise can be beneficial for midfield players who might need to learn how to defend and play quickly on the counter.
- The concept of counter-pressing is rooted in quick transitional play from an aggressive defence to a quick counter-attack. This exercise works on pressing together as a unit which is necessary to provide a team with a chance to transition quickly.

Session: Defending in a High Press 3 (1-1-1-2)

- **Recommended Time:** 20 minutes
- **Number of Players:** 6+

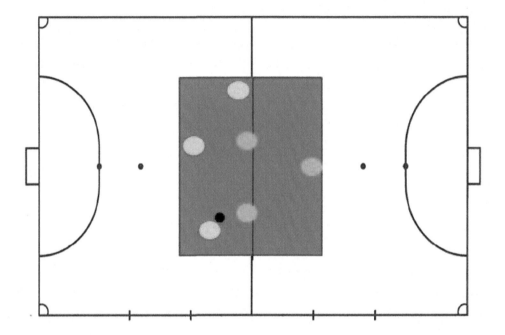

Focus of Session: Movement, working as a unit, pressing and transitions.

Objectives: To introduce the role of the screener to the high press.

Organisation: Two teams of three play against each other in a 20x10m grid. To score a goal a team must stop the ball on the opposite line. When out of possession, two of the defending team must drop off to the halfway line with the other member of the team dropping off to the line that they are defending. The defenders can rotate as a three but must always have one person on their own goal line. The player on the goal line – the screener – can stop passes through the middle. If the attackers break the line of the first two defenders then the screener can come off his line to apply pressure but may not retreat back. Instead the other two defenders must retreat back to their own goal line.

48

Coaching Factors:

- The first two players must try and press as the front two players in a 1-1-1-2.
- Defenders should alter their body shape accordingly, to force play down one side.
- The three defensive players should rotate their positions depending upon where the ball is. The position of screener should always be refilled.
- Defenders should adjust their position to limit passing options for their opponents, focusing particularly on preventing passes from being played through the middle of their defence.
- The defenders' first priority is to stop the ball from being played forward. The more the opposition pass the ball sideways the greater the opportunity to regain possession there is.

Progression Ideas:

- Increase the size of the area.
- Add goals to enable the defenders to counter-attack.
- Overload the three defending players by adding in a fourth attacker.

Links to Football:

- Constant rotations in football mean that defenders need to understand when to track their opponent and when to pass him on or exchange him with another defender.
- Different contexts demand different defending styles. Players need to understand when to press and when to delay the attackers.
- Although a 1-1-1-2 system of pressing relates to all positions on the football field (goalkeeper-defenders-midfielders-strikers), this exercise can be used to work on the defensive shape of a midfield three where one player is in a holding role.
- Rotating defensive positions enables a team to maintain their line. This prevents the opposition from gaining territorial advantage.

Session: Defending Man for Man 1

- **Recommended Time:** 20 minutes
- **Number of Players:** 8+

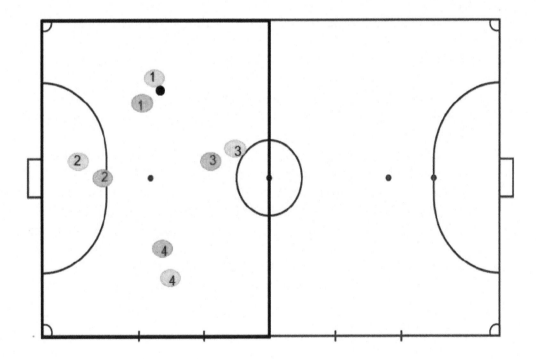

Focus of Session: Movement, pressing, tackling and transitions.

Objectives: To introduce the concept of man-to-man marking.

Organisation: Players are split into two teams of four. Each person within the team is given a number from one to four and then matches up with the same number from the other team. This is the only player on the opposition team that they can tackle, i.e. number ones can only tackle number ones. The two teams play against each other across the width of half a court. To score a goal a team must stop the ball on the opposition's line.

Coaching Factors:

- Defenders should get touch-tight to their opponents.
- Their body shape should be side-on but aggressive.
- Defenders need to understand when to get tight to opponents and when to tuck inside the court to cover their teammates and prevent forward passes.
- Work on recovery runs to minimise the threat of defending outnumbered.
- When tracking a man, running backwards allows you to see both the ball and the player. Defenders should attempt to run backwards when tracking their man whenever possible.

Progression Ideas:

- Place mini goals in either corner to enable teams to score by either stopping the ball on the line, or scoring into a goal.
- Teams can score by stopping the ball on the line or by making ten passes. This will increase the intensity of the defending.
- Add a floating player who plays for whichever team is in possession. This floater can only play in the defensive half of the team in possession.

Links to Football:

- Players need to have an awareness at all times of exactly where on the field the ball and their opponents are.
- Football is a game of individual battles all over the pitch. This exercise is all about not getting beaten by your opponent.
- This exercise also relates well to wide players and full backs, who must follow attacking players if balls are played past them.

Session: Defending Man for Man 2

- **Recommended Time:** 20 minutes
- **Number of Players:** 14+

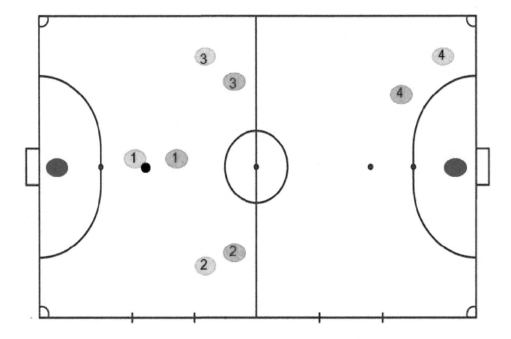

Focus of Session: Pressing and tackling.

Objectives: To develop man-to-man marking.

Organisation: Players are split into two teams and are assigned numbers (numbered bibs are recommended). Players can only tackle an opponent with the corresponding number, i.e. number ones can only tackle number ones on the opposing team. The two teams play a normal 5v5 game on a full futsal court. Although players can only tackle the player with their corresponding number on the other team, they may also block shots and intercept passes made by any other opposition players.

Coaching Factors:

- Ensure that defenders make themselves as big as possible. This will intimidate attackers.
- When closing down a man, defenders should start off with a flat body shape, moving side-on as they get closer to the player with the ball.
- If an opponent is travelling with the ball a defender should attack the front of his hips as this will likely be the position of the ball. Press aggressively (especially on triggers).
- Even if opponents do not have the ball defenders should get tight to them.

Progression Ideas:

- Split the pitch in half. In a team's defensive half, the same rules apply, but when defending in the opposition's half, players may tackle anyone.
- Ten consecutive passes count as a goal.

Links to Football:

- Players need to be able to see the man they are defending and the ball at all times.
- When defending, players must get tight enough to restrict their opponents' space, but not so tight that they can easily be turned.

Session: Defending Man for Man Follow Through

- **Recommended Time:** 20 minutes
- **Number of Players:** 10+

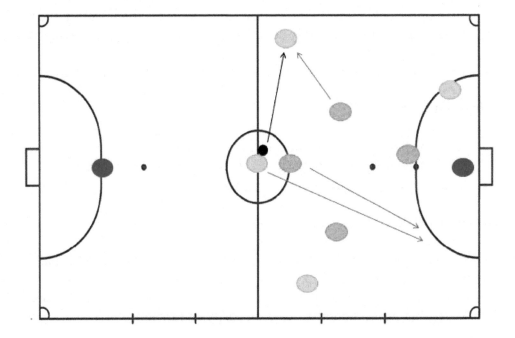

Focus of Session: Pressing, transitions, covering and working as a unit.

Objectives: To incorporate man-to-man marking within the diamond shape.

Organisation: Two teams play a normal futsal game on a full court. Both teams initially set up in their (respective) diamond shapes when defending. The halfway line is used as a reference. Once the ball is played over the halfway line the defence should transition from a diamond shape to following their man. This tactic is known as half court follow through.

Coaching Factors:

- Players are responsible for following their man once they pass the ball.
- It is important to shut off passing options to the middle of the court.
- Defenders need to understand when to go tight to their man and when to go looser. This depends on the pressure on the ball.
- Defenders not only have to follow their man but also cover the most dangerous areas on the pitch.
- Defenders can pass runners on to their fellow defenders to allow for more efficient zonal defending. Communication is vital for this to be done.
- All defensive decisions must be made in relation to the defensive pressure that is on the ball

Progression Ideas:

- One team plays in a zonal diamond the whole time and the other defends man-to-man.
- Take out the goal at each end and play line ball. This makes it harder to defend.
- Play an attack versus defence game on half a court. The attackers get ten attacks to score. If they score then the game resets and they get another ten attacks. This puts the defending team under pressure to make sure they do not concede. The defending team must defend in a half-court follow through. If they do not concede a goal in ten attacks then the attackers and defenders switch around.

Links to Football:

- Football players need to understand when to man-mark and when to pass on players.
- When playing against a false 9 or an attacking midfielder, centre backs and centre midfielders will have to decide whether to track their man or pass him on.
- Being able to pass on or track efficiently enables protection of zone 14 without exposing yourselves defensively.
- Players need to assess risk – whether the man or an area is more dangerous – and act accordingly.

Chapter 4: Attacking

There are no players on a futsal court whose sole job is to defend. All players defend as a unit, and all players attack as a unit. Positions are not fixed. Although a player may begin as a winger, he is just as likely to find himself as a pivot or cierre during a game. Players must not only be able to deny opponents space and prevent goal-scoring opportunities, but also be comfortable creating opportunities and shooting at goal.

Over in Brazil, where futsal has been practised for over 80 years, football is a fluid, dynamic game where players play across all areas of the pitch. Centre backs roam forward into attack, full backs cut inside to the number 10 position and forwards rotate with holding midfielders. Whereas players in England are confined to a position as early as the age of 8, their counterparts in Brazil are generally allowed to play freely. Brazilian players only tend to specialise in certain positions from the age of 13.

This limitation on young English players has repercussions. Players who are ushered into defensive spots never learn to attack; players who are selected as strikers rarely learn how to defend. As they get older, and the demands of attacking and defending as a unit increase, they fall by the wayside.

The need to play in a number of positions is becoming essential in the modern game of football. Just one look at Pep Guardiola's Bayern Munich emphasises this. A player such as Philip Lahm is comfortable playing across a number of positions. Within a game Lahm rotates and interchanges with his teammates, finding himself across a range of positions throughout the game. This is a fluid form of football, allowing managers to use a wide range of tactics in the 90 minutes.

The technical demands on certain positions have increased as the 11-a-side game has modernised. Full backs must now be equally capable of attacking and defending; centre backs must be able to play out from the back and start attacks; and goalkeepers set up attacks and act as sweepers.

Futsal encourages this adaptability, developing technically and tactically astute players for the 11-a-side game. Amongst the key principles of attacking in futsal are movement, interchange and rotation. To find space to play in a tight area, players must interchange with each other. This disrupts defenders and opens up passing lines for the player in possession of the ball.

'Pass and move' has always been a key concept within football. Rotations and interchanges, however, are becoming embedded within the modern game. The invention of the false 9, the increase in teams playing with three central midfield players and the more intelligent 'pressing game' employed by teams has ensured that players must rotate to escape pressure and find success.

This chapter introduces three of the most common rotations in futsal: rotating as a 2-2, 3-1 and 4-0. Within each of these rotations, speed of play and speed of movement are essential. The ball must be passed firmly to disrupt the defence as effectively as possible. If movement is too slow, the player in possession will have too few options; too quick and he will not only be limited, but will more than likely have less space to work in. The player in possession is also vital. They must make decisions quickly. The aim of these rotations is to create enough space for a player to get a shot at goal or to isolate a player in an advanced position. If this player receives the ball, he should be encouraged to attempt to beat his marker.

As speed of play is essential, all training should be carried out at match intensity. This is also important when counter-attacking – another constantly developing feature of the modern game. At the 2014 World Cup, 34 of the 171 goals scored were from counter-attacks. Real Madrid scored 33% of their goals in the 2013 UEFA Champions League from counter-attacks. The reduced number of players in a futsal game means that teams are regularly able to attack their opponent with an overload. To do this, they must transition with speed from defence to attack. Decisions need to be made quickly to make the most of the numerical advantage.

This chapter also details how to make the most of counter-attacks. Sophisticated methods of defending such as gegenpressing and the deep zonal diamond are built on the foundations of counter-attacks. As soon as the ball is won, a team must commit to the attack. If the action is not finished, however, they become susceptible to the counter-counter. Herein lies the beauty of futsal – the waves of counter-attacks, demanding numerous quick decisions over the course of a training session. Transferred to the 11-a-side game there are obvious benefits.

The sessions detailed in the following pages are not rigid; they merely act as guidance. Players should be encouraged to fill the spaces advised on the pitch, but should also be encouraged to be creative, innovative, and to enjoy having possession of the ball. Most importantly of all, all players should be encouraged to play everywhere. Try your centre back in a pivot position. Have your full backs interchanging in central areas as a cierre. Invite your goalkeeper to powerplay. The technical rewards will be enormous.

Session: Finishing Using the Pivot - Pivot Wars

- **Recommended Time:** 20 minutes
- **Number of Players:** 10+

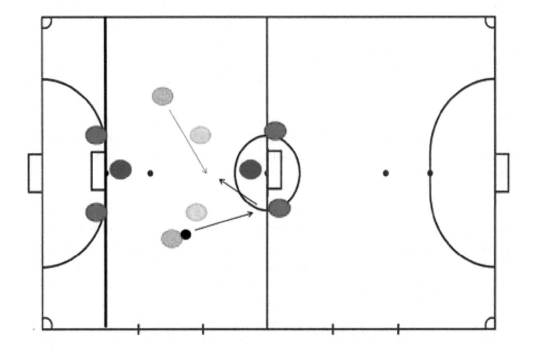

Focus of Session: Passing, movement, control and finishing.

Objectives: To play into the pivot – who sets back for a first time finish – as quickly as possible.

Organisation: In an area from the D to the halfway line, with goals at either end, two teams play against each other in a 2v2. There is a floating player – the pivot – positioned at either side of each goal. The goalkeeper begins the practice by rolling the ball to a player on his team. This player then looks to score as quickly as possible. They can use the floating players to get a set back to help them score, but these players are limited to two touches. If they receive a set back from a pivot, they must score with a first time finish.

Coaching Factors:

- Play forward as early as possible.
- Rotate to create space and engineer shooting opportunities.
- Feinting and checking is important to lose markers.
- If the ball is played into the pivot, players should change their follow up runs to lose defenders, helping them to finish first time.
- Finish the action to prevent being countered on.

Progression Ideas:

- This session can be adapted so the focus is on physical returns. Increasing the time that players work for will help.
- Goalkeepers can join in to create an overload.
- One of the floating players can drop inside the pitch by a metre to open up the opportunity for a back post finish.
- Play 3v3.

Links to Football:

- The penalty area can often get congested, with lots of defensive pressure. In these scenarios, quick one and two touch finishes are effective.
- Number 10s and box-to-box midfielders will play the ball into the forward and follow their pass for a first time finish from the set back. This exercise develops the movements required to lose markers.
- Positive forward play when possible is needed to break lines and dictate the tempo.

Session: Developing Finishing in Key Areas - The Money-Maker

- **Recommended Time:** 20 minutes
- **Number of Players:** 12+

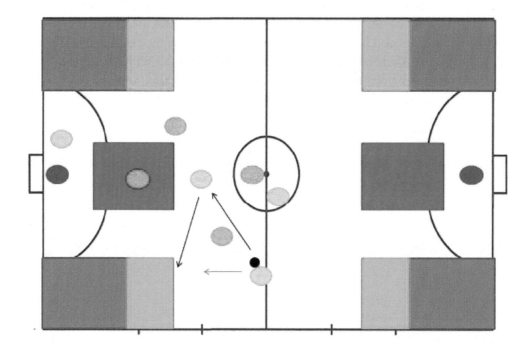

Focus of Session: Passing, movement and finishing.

Objectives: To develop finishing in key areas of a futsal court, recognising when the opportunity to finish is on, and when to take the risk.

Organisation: Two teams of four outfield players and a goalkeeper play a normal game across a full court. Key areas, where the best scoring opportunities can be created, are marked on the court with flat cones, as shown. Teams are awarded one goal for scoring normally. Two goals are given if a wall pass is made into the green area before scoring a goal. Two goals are also given if the ball is shot from the blue area to the back post for a back post finish. Finally, three goals are awarded if the ball is played in the red area and the team scores when in this same area.

Coaching Factors:

- Players need to understand that when in the blue area it is best to set the ball back and not to cross. Crossing from this area often results in a counter-attack for the other team as the goalkeeper or defenders can easily gather the ball and play forward quickly. Though this factor differs from football, the concept that poor crosses can lead to being countered on remains.
- Recognise when passing opportunities are on to the back post. Having somebody on the back post opens up more passing lines and affects the goalkeeper.
- The presence of this player means that players in possession should 'shoot to miss'. If aimed at the back post, this increases the chances of scoring and reduces the chance of being countered on.
- Always finish the action to prevent being countered on.
- To score in the red zone, players need to work the ball with defence-splitting passes. These are high risk but come with high reward.
- Players need to understand the type of pass they play to allow the receiver to finish accordingly. For example, in the red zone, where the receiver is unlikely to have time and space, they must finish first time. The set back should therefore be a slow pass with the sole of the foot.
- When playing the ball to the back post, the passer should put plenty of pace on the pass. The receiver will then merely need to redirect the ball with any body part possible for a first time finish.

Progression Ideas:

- Reward combination play with goals.
- If players misplace passes or miss the target they have to drop out of the game, making it a 4v3. This will create more opportunities to practise the topic. Players are allowed to re-join the session if the opposing team score a goal.
- Have one team play with one less player. This will make their attacks more realistic to football, where attackers are usually outnumbered by defenders.

Links to Football:

- At first glance, this session appears to be very futsal specific. When broken down, however, the benefits to football become apparent.
- This links in with players penetrating opposition defenders on the edge of their 18-yard box.
- The set back relates to a forward setting the ball for a midfielder to run onto for a first time finish.
- The pass to the back post is a line-breaking pass which can split the back four, and aims to get midfield runners or forwards to run on to and finish first time.
- To score goals, players need to risk passes. Penetrating the last line of defence is essential to creating chances.
- Knowing the types of pass to allow players to finish is essential. Recognising triggers and the context of the game impacts decision-making in choosing the correct kind of pass. Knowing which passing technique to use at a certain point in the game is essential (and applies to all players).

Session: Counter-Attacking 1 - Box to Boxing

- **Recommended Time**: 15 minutes
- **Number of Players**: 5+

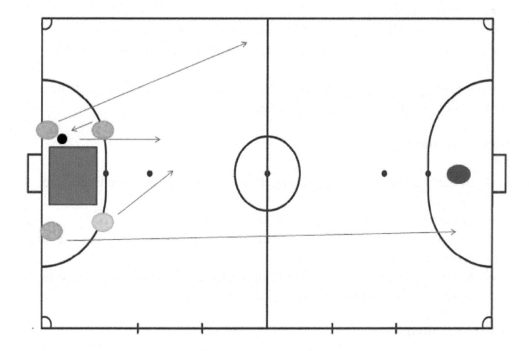

Focus of Session: Travelling with the ball and finishing.

Objectives: For players to counter-attack as soon as they regain possession.

Organisation: In one of the Ds, four outfield players set up, with one player in each corner of a 5x5 metre box. Opposite them in the far goal there is one goalkeeper. The four players pass the ball between themselves in the square, staying in their allocated corners. At any moment, one of these players can decide to stop the ball with the sole of their foot. This is the trigger movement. Once the ball is stopped in this manner, the player opposite the ball becomes the defender. The other three players attack, though the player who stopped the ball cannot dribble the ball out of the 5x5m area. Instead, another player must come to collect the ball and attack the far goal in a 3v1 counter-attack. Once this attack is completed, the players reorganise in the square and begin the practice again.

Coaching Factors:

- Speed of play is essential. The ball must move quickly at all times.
- Keeping the ball in central areas when attacking gives the player in possession more passing options.
- Engage the defender.
- One player should go high to break the line of the defender.
- Try to shoot toward the back post, where the third attacker should be positioned.
- Finishing the action is essential. If shots are weak then opponents can easily launch counter-attacks of their own.

Progression Ideas:

- In the 5x5 metre square, the player to the left becomes a defender once the ball is stopped.
- Passes in the square must be one touch only.
- When attacking, limit the number of passes the players can take, i.e. must score in less than five passes.
- Make it a 2v2, rather than a 3v1, i.e. both players on the opposite side to where ball is stopped become defenders.

Links to Football:

- The speed with which counter-attacks occur in futsal is faster than in football.
- As the game is played in a tighter area, spotting the right trigger and acting accordingly is essential.
- Players with the ball need to travel at pace to engage the defender.
- This drill improves decision-making. More effective decisions will lead to more successful counter-attacks.
- If sitting deep or using a system of gegenpressing, counter-attacks are essential. Because of this, there is a great emphasis on quick counters and effective decision-making.
- Re-countering counter-attacks is becoming more prevalent in football. Finishing the action prevents counter-attacks from being countered.

Session: Counter-Attacking 2 - Counter the Counter

- **Recommended Time:** 20 minutes
- **Number of Players:** 10+

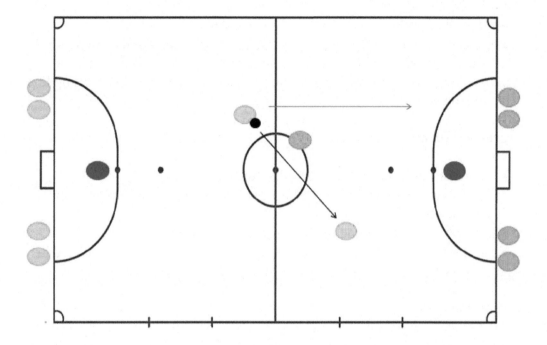

Focus of Session: Movement, travelling with the ball and finishing.

Objectives: To practise different counter-attacking situations initiated by the goalkeeper.

Organisation: Players split evenly between two teams, with one goalkeeper playing for each team. Teams must have at least four outfield players who line up behind the goal. The green team start the practice by attacking their opponents 2v1. They play to a finish. When they have taken a shot and the action is over, the player who took the shot touches the goal line whilst the blue's goalkeeper plays the ball out to two blue attackers. They attack the green player who did not take the shot in a 2v1, with the green player who did take the shot acting as a recovery defender. Once this action is over, the greens attack the blues in a 3v2, initiated by their goalkeeper. The exercise continues in this manner until the game eventually becomes a 4v4.

Coaching Factors:

- Travel with the ball at speed.
- Always pass the ball quickly.
- Play at match intensity.
- Finish the action.
- Travel centrally with the ball to keep passing options high.
- Attacking players should support the man on the ball by making forward runs. One player can support in a slightly advanced position to the side and one should attempt to get onto the back post to open up a passing line and draw the goalkeeper out.

Progression Ideas:

- Players can come on from the substitute gates.
- Keep the game as a 2v1 so that the player who takes the shot does not recover but instead drops out.
- Keep the game 3v2 and remove the recovery player.
- Limit the time allowed for each attack, i.e. attacks must be completed in ten seconds.

Links to Football:

- The speed at which players travel with the ball and make decisions when counter-attacking can be the difference between teams winning and losing at an elite level.
- The increased number of teams using block defences in football has led to a greater emphasis on counter-attacking.
- A block defence denies space and aims to exploit space that opponents leave behind themselves. Counter-attacking is essential for success with this tactic.

Session: Counter-Attacking 3 - Make it Count

- **Recommended Time:** 20 minutes
- **Number of Players:** 10+

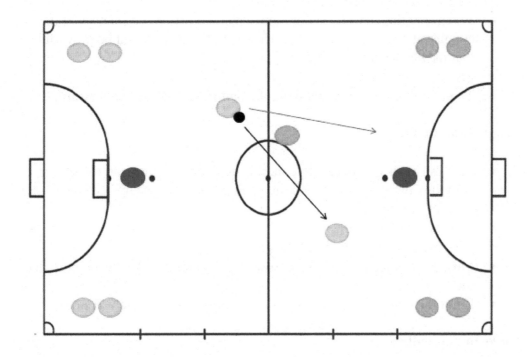

Focus of Session: Movement, travelling with the ball and finishing.

Objectives: To counter-attack quickly and create finishes in 2v1 situations.

Organisation: The goals are moved forward so they are on the edge of each D. Two teams are split evenly, with each team having at least four outfield players. These players set up in each corner of their touchline. The goalkeeper begins the practice by throwing the ball out to one of the greens, who attack the blue player in a 2v1. Once a green player takes a shot, they drop out and the blue goalkeeper plays the ball to a blue player waiting in the corner. This player joins the attack to make it a transition 2v1 in the opposite direction. The exercise continues in this manner.

Coaching Factors:

- Move quickly in possession to attack the defender.
- The second attacker should try to get on the back post whilst keeping a passing line open for the player in possession.
- Run with the ball rather than dribble.
- When shooting, try and shoot high. This will lessen the chances of the counter-attack being countered. However, the shot should be powerful so that the keeper cannot catch the ball.
- Play at match intensity.
- The first thought when receiving the ball should always be forward.

Progression Ideas:

- Play 2v1 with a recovery defender. Instead of dropping out, the player who took the shot must touch the goalpost before chasing back as a recovery defender.
- Increase the size of the area.
- Alter the starting position of the players.
- Limit the number of passes allowed in a counter-attack, i.e. no more than three.
- Limit the time allowed for attacks, i.e. must be done in ten seconds.

Links to Football:

- This exercise has huge links to teams playing with a block defence. In this tactic, players must understand when to take the risk and explode in a counter-attack. This knowledge comes from the assessment of triggers.
- Counter-attacks must be quick and efficient to be successful.
- When counter-attacking, actions must be finished to prevent the attacking team from being countered by the opposition.
- When teams are pressing high and regaining possession high up the pitch, they often have an overload in the transition. The first decision in this transition is so important in the modern game.

Session: Decision-Making in Possession - No Rest for the Wicked

- **Recommended Time:** 20 minutes

- **Number of Players:** 12+

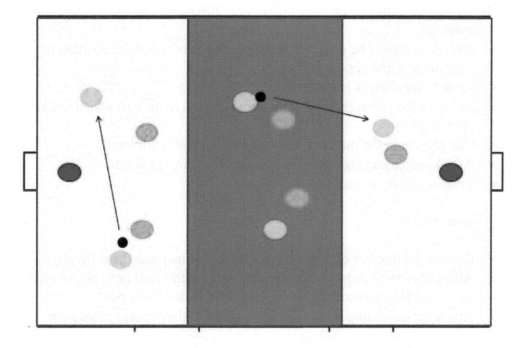

Focus of Session: Passing, movement and feinting to receive.

Objectives: For players to understand when to retain the ball under pressure and when to pass forward.

Organisation: A full court is split evenly into thirds. The first and second thirds are both 2v2, and the final third is 1v1. The goalkeeper plays to his defenders, who then play forward into the next third when able to do so. The ball must go through all of the thirds before the pivot in the final third can score a goal.

Once the ball has been played from the first third to the middle third, the goalkeeper gets another ball and plays it into the two defenders, even though the first ball is still in the middle third. It is therefore possible for the attacking team to be playing with a ball in each third. Once the attacking team has had a set number of chances, or amount of time, the teams switch over with the defenders becoming the attackers.

69

Coaching Factors:

- Play forward as quickly and with as much quality as possible.
- If you cannot play forward – i.e. passing lines are blocked or the forward players are still working with a ball in their third – look to keep the ball and retain possession until you can.
- Work as a team to look after possession. Rotations and interchanges are essential.
- Decisions should be dictated by positions on court and the position of your players and opponents.
- Look to combine if possible.
- Embrace the pressure. Do not be afraid to receive the ball whilst under intense pressure.
- Can players in the middle turn on the ball and play forward?
- Attacking players should try and get shots off in 1v1 situations.
- Train at match intensity.

Progression Ideas:

- Change the number of players in each third to increase the difficulty.
- Allow players to drop in and out of zones to underload or overload areas, i.e. if you play forward into a zone you can follow your pass.
- Allow the defending team to counter-attack if they regain possession.

Links to Football:

- Players need to understand when to play with purposeful possession.
- If the ball is played forward too soon then possession is more likely to be overturned. Understanding the context of the game and recognising triggers makes attacks more effective.
- When playing out from the back, this knowledge is essential. The modern centre back needs to be comfortable on the ball and able to make effective passes to begin attacks. This drill helps them develop their decision-making and the quality of pass into more advanced positions.
- Central midfielders need to be able to receive the ball from their centre back even when they are under pressure. The tight area and close pressure from defenders in this drill helps develop this ability. If possible, they should look to turn in order to play forward.
- Forwards regularly isolate defenders in 1v1 scenarios in the final third. They must be devastating with their play.

Session: Fly Keeper - I Believe I Can Fly

- **Recommended Time:** 20 minutes
- **Players:** 12+

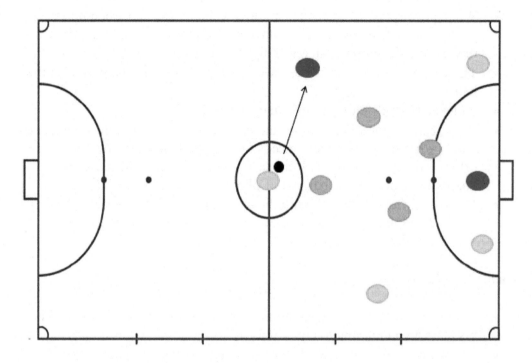

Focus of Session: Passing, control and finishing.

Objectives: For players to learn how to play with a fly keeper.

Organisation: Two teams play a normal game. When the team in possession gets into the attacking half, the goalkeeper joins them, playing in the attacking half as well. This is known as a *powerplay*. It is imperative that the goalkeeper remains in the attacking half, as he cannot have the ball more than once in his own half in any given possession. When in the opponent's half, the goalkeeper is able to touch the ball as often as he wishes. If the defending team win the ball, they are able to counter-attack and score.

Coaching Factors:

- Ball speed is vital. Passes must be quick in order to disrupt defenders.
- Dribbling past players negates the numerical advantage. Focus on quick passes between players.
- When powerplaying, teams must know when to risk and when to retain possession. The numerical advantage means that risk often translates to reward, but the empty goal also heightens the risk.
- There should always be at least two passing options for the player on the ball.
- Patience is key. Enjoy possession of the ball.
- If the team in possession comes under great pressure from the defenders, a player – not the goalkeeper – needs to drop deep into their own half to offer a safe passing option. If this is not possible, then the player in possession can kick the ball out of play. This should be the last resort.
- Work on different systems with the attacking overload. These include 1-2-2, 2-1-2 and three in a line. In these systems, players do not rotate but instead hold their position.

Progression Ideas:

- If a team is finding the concept too difficult, a player must drop out when his team are defending to create a 5v3.
- Allow the powerplay to take place with a goalkeeper in goal – as well as one flying – for the team in possession. This goalkeeper is not allowed to leave the D. The insurance of a goalkeeper will encourage the team in possession to be more positive with their passing and explore different options.
- The fly keeper is an excellent tactic for scoring goals. Time how many goals a team can score in a set number of minutes.
- The fly keeper is also a good way of keeping possession. Time how long a team can keep possession of the ball using a fly keeper.

Links to Football:

- The modern goalkeeper must be just as comfortable with the ball at their feet as they are with it in their hands. Working on this drill from a young age will improve a goalkeeper's ability to play with the ball at his feet, encouraging him to start attacks from deep.
- Goalkeepers often have to play out from the back against an underload of defenders. Playing forward with confidence under pressure to break

passing lines is required.
- From time to time, outfield players will have to play against teams who have had a man sent off. When doing so, they must break down their opponents by moving the ball quickly and understanding when to risk and when to retain possession.
- Teams should enjoy possessions. Patience is key.

Session: Developing Forward Combination Play - Don't Wait; Create

- **Recommended Time:** 15 minutes

- **Number of Players:** 4+

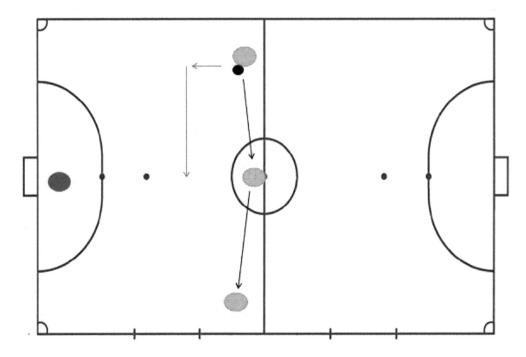

Focus of Session: Passing and movement.

Objectives: For players to learn how to move as a three in a basic rotation. To develop an understanding of the parallel pass, wall pass or helping pass and when to use them.

Organisation: Working in one half of the pitch, players set up evenly on the halfway line, with two wingers and one middle man. This is an unopposed activity. The goalkeeper begins the exercise by throwing the ball out to one of the two wingers. The winger on the ball then plays the ball into the middle man. The first movement of the passer, after playing the ball, is forward. He feints that he is going to move down the line. He then comes inside into central areas. Whilst this movement is going on, the middle player passes the ball to the opposite winger. This winger now has an option of passing the ball forward to the winger who made the initial movement. He can play the ball to him using a parallel pass, where the ball is scooped down the line for the winger to run on to; a helping pass, where the winger plays the ball centrally and follows his pass, getting a small roll to one side allowing him to finish first time; or a wall pass where the ball is bounced into the central area and back out for the second winger to run onto. Alternatively, the second winger can play the ball back across court to the middle man, who rotates out toward the vacated winger position. If the ball is passed forward, this middle man then runs forward to get on the back post.

Coaching Factors:

- The winger who receives the ball needs to rotate centrally to create an overload – pass in the middle, move to the middle.
- The first movement in any of the winger's rotations should be forward. This will make the defender think they are making a direct forward run.
- Synchronise movements with the position of the ball on the court, i.e. there is no point in overloading central areas if the middle man is still in possession of the ball.
- Players waiting to receive the ball should check. In a game, this will affect their marker, giving them more time and space on the ball once they receive it. Check one yard to make five yards.
- A player's body shape must be open to receive the ball.
- Attackers should be in a position where the player in possession will give them the ball.
- Understand the purpose of the different combination passes.
- Speed of play is essential. Quicker passes will disrupt defenders more easily.
- Passes need to have enough quality to allow the receiver to play the ball with one or two touches when in key areas. For example, the wall pass into wide areas needs to be weighted to allow for a first time strike to the back post.
- The ball does not have to go forward the first time the winger receives it. If they wish, they can reset the formation and begin the rotation again.

Progression Ideas:

- Put in a defender to press the player who rotates into the middle. This will affect their decision as to whether to use a helping pass, parallel pass, or wall pass.
- Split the area in half, with one defender defending the top half and another defending the half with the goal.

Links to Football:

- When playing in tight areas such as zone 14, players need to know when to keep the ball and when to penetrate opponents by playing forward.
- If players are able to retain possession whilst facing forward it will be of benefit. Facing forward when receiving the ball allows the player to see the picture in front of him and pass forward if it is on. This exercise allows the player to use a helping pass to retain possession whilst facing forward.
- With these combination plays, players can recognise the opportunity to exploit defences which are unbalanced in the areas the ball is in.
- Players need to be comfortable on the ball in tight areas even when they are pressed.
- Rotations and interchanges are essential in forward positions to create space, penetrate lines of defence and exploit opponents.

Session: Combining to Play Forward in a 3-1 Formation - Transfer Window

- **Recommended Time:** 20 minutes
- **Number of Players:** 9+

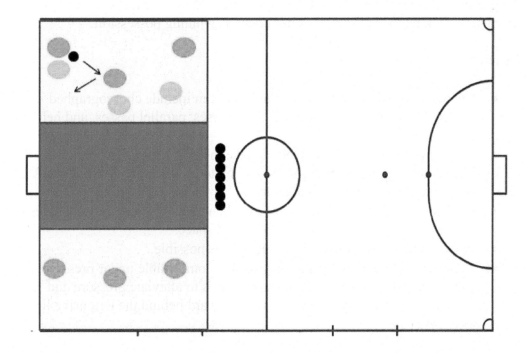

Focus of Session: Passing and movement.

Objectives: To develop players' understanding of when and where to combine in order to exploit opponents and create an overload.

Organisation: A 15x30m area is marked out on court and split evenly to make three thirds. Players are split into three teams of three, with each team occupying an area of the pitch. This is a transfer game, with the team in the middle defending.

The coach initiates the practice by playing a pass into one of the two teams in an end zone. Once a player touches the ball, the defenders are able to enter the zone belonging to the team in possession. The team in possession is allowed to transfer the ball over to the other team as soon as they receive the ball, but this is classed as a safe forward pass and no score is made. To score a goal, the team in possession must either perform attacking combination plays, such as wall passes, helping passes, or parallel passes, or run with the ball into the middle third and then pass it forward.

If the defending team wins possession they can turn and play the ball to the other team at the opposite end. The team that loses possession becomes the new defenders. If the defending team do not make this pass, however, they stay as defenders. Kicking the ball out does not count as winning possession.

Coaching Factors:

- Encourage clever combination play. This can include choreographed moves during possession, such as wall passes, parallel passes, and helping passes.
- Players need to understand when to take the risk once an overload has been created in the correct way and when to try and play forward in a safe way to retain possession in high areas.
- Decisions need to be made regarding when to combine as a two or three and when to travel with the ball to exploit space.
- Players should face forward as regularly as possible.
- Create an environment where players feel comfortable under pressure. Emphasise how players can make overloads to alleviate pressure and remind them that they are able to play forward behind the defensive line as a 'safe pass'.

Progression Ideas:

- Once players have travelled with the ball or successfully combined and entered the middle third they then have to attack the opposite end and stop the ball on the end line to score a goal. The three players in this zone become a second set of defenders who attempt to prevent the attacking team from scoring.
- Put a goal two metres past the end line. Once players travel with the ball or successful combination play has taken place, the attacking team can try and score past the goalkeeper in the opposite goal.

Links to Football:

- Players need to be comfortable when playing under pressure – not only to keep control of the ball, but also in terms of their decision-making. Players must make good decisions at all times on the pitch, regardless of the pressure they are under.

- When attacking, teams need to break defensive lines to be successful.
- If the pass forward is not possible, teams need to rotate to maintain possession.
- In this drill, the team in the opposite zone are not resting. Instead, they are constantly moving to open up passing lines. This mirrors the work on the numbers 9 and 10, who need to move to open up passing lines forward.
- In certain moments in a game, however, the number 9 and 10 will need to stay away from their midfielders to allow them space to work in. This drill develops play between midfielders for such instances.

Session: Combination Play - Linking the Chain

- **Recommended Time:** 20 minutes
- **Number of Players:** 12+

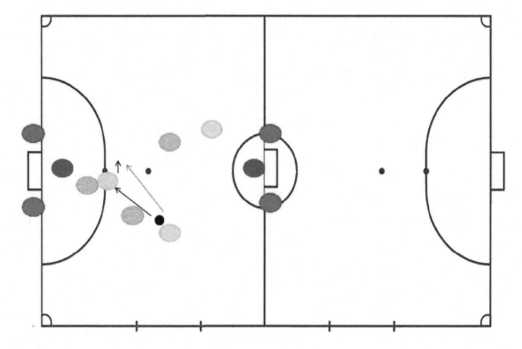

Focus of Session: Passing, movement and finishing.

Objectives: To know when to combine with a forward player and when to play as a three, with the objective of scoring goals.

Organisation: A directional game is played in a 20x20 metre area with goals at either end. There are two floating players beside each goal. In the area, two teams play in a 3v3, with a goalkeeper in each goal. One team begins the practice by receiving the ball from their goalkeeper. They then attempt to combine to play forward and score a goal. They can use the floaters positioned next to the goal to do so. These players set the ball back for the team in possession to shoot.

Coaching Factors:

- Look to combine as soon as possible.
- Make sure ball speed is high to make defending harder.
- Players should have a good first touch to secure the ball and set up play as quickly as possible.
- Players should quickly exploit the space in front of them.
- Encourage attacking players to rotate to create overloads in certain areas of the pitch.
- If it is on, play forward into one of the two floaters.
- If the ball does go to a floater, the attacking team need to support the play quickly to give passing options and create goal-scoring opportunities.

Progression Ideas:

- The floating players can join in on the back post to score.
- The floating player can work down their side of the pitch to the halfway line, creating overloads.
- The floating player can join in with play once the ball has been passed to them. If the team then loses possession they must return to the outside of the pitch.
- Play three-minute games. The winning team gets to stay on; the losing team switches with the floating players.
- Change the shape of a pitch to a diamond. This gives the floater a greater area to work in.
- Floating players only have one touch.
- To score, players must finish with one touch.

Links to Football:

- Forward players combine in, and around, the 18-yard box to try and score goals.
- This drill works on a player's decision-making: do they travel with the ball to penetrate the defence, combine with a forward player, a fellow midfield player, set up an attack, or shoot from distance?
- Making effective decisions based on the context of the game – e.g. position of the opponents – is essential for success in football. In the tighter area of a futsal court, and with the extra speed of a futsal ball, the emphasis on effective decision-making is magnified.

Session: Developing Combination Play and Making Rotations Fluid - Over the Underload

- **Recommended Time:** 20 minutes

- **Number of Players:** 12+

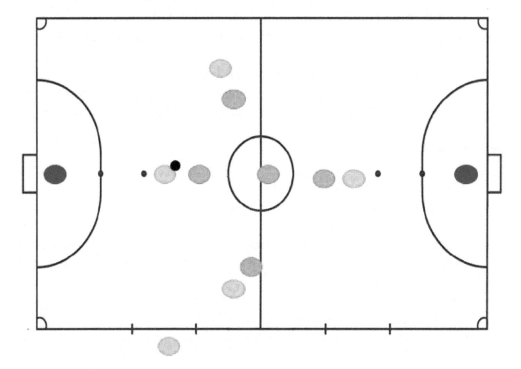

Focus of Session: Passing, movement and finishing.

Objectives: To continue to develop players' combination play and understanding of the need to rotate.

Organisation: A normal game takes place across a full court. The team in possession has the normal four outfield players, but the defending team is allowed an extra player to create a defensive overload with five outfield players. If the defending team regains possession then one of their players must drop out of the game, and the team that lost possession is allowed an extra player on court to defend.

Coaching Factors:

- The team in possession is working against a defensive overload. As such, they need to attempt to rotate to create overloads of their own.
- To do this, ball speed should remain high at all times.
- The team in possession should attempt to use parallel passes, wall passes, and helping passes when possible.
- If a player has no passing options when on the ball they should remain in possession until an option becomes open.
- In this situation, the player can alter his surroundings by travelling with the ball to break defensive lines.
- If a player comes under pressure from a defender, teammates should not run off. Instead, they should drop to support the pressed player with a safe pass or get closer to the player and use combination play to escape the pressure.
- Players are overloaded; they need to be brave in possession and with their movements.
- Players should always be moving to create space. The defensive overload makes this factor even more essential.

Progression Ideas:

- Players must enter and exit via the substitute gate only.
- Points are awarded for different types of line-breaking combinations.
- If the team in possession crosses the halfway line, the defending team either loses a player or gains another player, depending on how difficult the coach wishes to make the session.
- Passing drop out – if a player losses possession they must drop out of the game until a transition happens.
- A player decides when to drop out on their own evaluation and decision-making. For example, if they play negatively when they could have combined, they should drop out. Failure to recognise poor decisions can be punished by the coach with the award of a free-kick for the other team or by giving a goal to the other team.

Links to Football:

- The ability to play against a defensive overload is essential in football. For example, and as discussed previously, when defending teams attempt to force opponents into certain areas where they can gain possession more easily.

- When playing against a defensive overload, players must remain calm and be brave on the ball. They need to embrace the pressure.
- If teams always train with even numbers or a numerical advantage then they will only ever be used to playing with even numbers or a numerical advantage when it comes to match day.
- When playing against a defensive overload, decisions need to be effective. Players have to understand when to risk possession and when to retain possession.
- When underloaded, it is often most effective to shorten distances between players to make combination play easier.
- This ability is crucial for midfield players who are learning how to play out of their own half, as well as how to retain possession high up the pitch in order to create opportunities and penetrate defences.

Session: Rotating as a Three

- **Recommended Time:** 20 minutes
- **Number of Players:** 6+

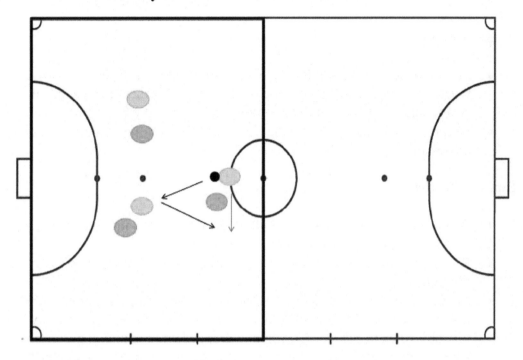

Focus of Session: Passing and movement.

Objectives: For players to understand the importance of rotating as a three.

Organisation: Across half a court, players play in a 3v3. To score a goal, they must stop the ball on the opposite line. If they do this, they turn and subsequently attack the opposite line.

Coaching Factors:

- Players must move the ball quickly to allow teammates to have as much time as possible on the ball.
- Look to play forward.
- After a pass a player should never stand still. They should look to rotate to create space, get on the ball, or affect the opposition.
- After passing, the first movement of the player rotating should always be forward.

85

- Players must rotate positions to create opportunities to keep possession, create overloads, and play forward.
- Teams should try to break their opponents' line of defence. To do this, players should rotate between, and past, their lines of defence.
- Teams should always look to combine in order to play forward.

Progression Ideas:

- Limit touches. For example, players can play with one touch but two touches to score (control and stop on the line). This increases technical development but also combination play under high pressure.
- Failure to rotate after playing the ball is a foul, resulting in a turnover of possession.

Links to Football:

- When playing against a 4-3-3, midfielders must rotate and interchange to affect the opposition and gain territorial advantage.
- Rotations to create overloads are essential in allowing teams to play forward.
- Central defensive midfielders need to dictate the tempo of games. In this drill, it is the task of the middle player to make decisions: when to play forward, when to risk passes, when to drop, when to maintain possession, when to rotate forward, when to start attacks, and when to restart attacks.
- Players need to understand when to be patient in possession and when to play forward. Tempo of play should always remain high.

Session: Rotating as a 2-2

- **Recommended Time:** 20 minutes
- **Number of Players:** 10+

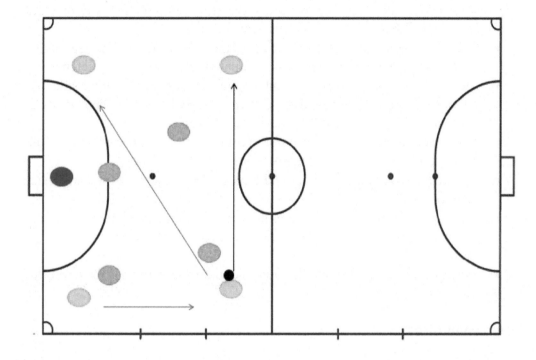

Focus of Session: Passing, movement and finishing.

Objectives: For players to understand how to rotate as a 2-2 - to open up defences.

Organisation: Teams are split evenly, playing in a 4v4. The defending team has a goalkeeper in goal. The defending team defends their own half in any system they wish. The goalkeeper begins the practice by throwing the ball to the attacking team, which is positioned on the halfway line. Using a 2-2 set-up, and rotating accordingly, they try to score as many goals as they can over a set number of chances (usually ten). Once they have completed their set number of attacks, the teams switch, with the defenders now attacking.

Coaching Factors:

- In this fixed 2-2 rotation, players will often end up where they started once the whole team has fully moved in a set way.
- In a 2-2 rotation, players move in a figure of eight. They start off by setting up in the shape of a box, with two players on the halfway line and two players in advanced positions near the goal.
- Once a player on the halfway line plays the ball across to their teammate, they make a diagonal forward run in an attempt to unlock the defence.
- If the passer makes this movement, the advanced player on their side of the box rotates back to re-fill the passer's original position. This opens up another passing line for the player in possession.
- The attacking team should attempt to rotate in this manner when possible. This rotation can happen as many times as a team wishes.
- Whenever possible, players should look to play forward, exploiting space and opponents.
- The player on the ball needs to understand when to pass forward, retain possession, travel with the ball, take on players 1v1, and shoot from range.
- The team in possession should look to exploit the middle of the court in their rotations.

Progression Ideas:

- Explore different rotations within a team's 2-2 set-up.
- Work on transitioning the whole team from a 2-2 to a 1-3.
- Bring in a breakout area for the defending team to attempt to go in when they win possession.

Links to Football:

- Players need to master the ball on the move from a young age. The 2-2 is a system where players continually move to get space and get on the ball.
- Decision-making is essential in football. This exercise enables players to understand when to play forward and when to keep the ball.
- Players need to constantly rotate and interchange in order to create space and open passing lines, especially in forward positions.

Session: Rotating as a 3-1 Using a False Pivot

- **Recommended Time:** 20 minutes
- **Number of Players:** 10+

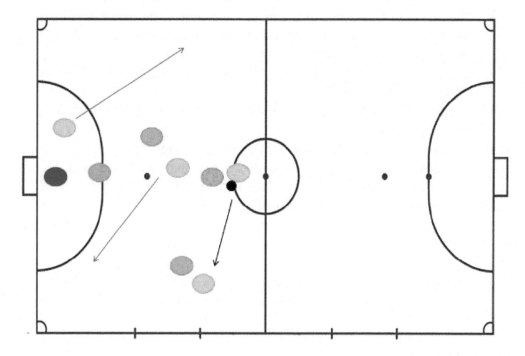

Focus of Session: Passing, movement and finishing.

Objectives: To teach players movement in a fluid rotation that creates overloads and disrupt defenders using a false pivot system.

Organisation: One team defends their own half in any system. The other team – the attackers – set up in a 3-1 formation in the same half. The goalkeeper begins the practice by throwing the ball to one of the three attacking players positioned on the halfway line. The attacking team tries to score as many goals as they can whilst rotating in a 3-1 formation with a false pivot. They are given a set number of chances – usually ten. Once these have been completed, the teams switch around, with the defending team now attacking.

Coaching Factors:

- In this system, a winger plays the ball and rotates into central areas to create an overload.

- If the winger does not get the ball, he rotates forward into an advanced position.
- Whilst this is happening, the pivot rotates back into the winger's original position. This rotation is done slower, with the pivot lingering in an advanced position in an attempt to get the ball in a high area.
- The player in the middle of the three – the cierre – holds his position, recycling the ball to each side and playing forward when possible. It is the cierre's job to dictate the tempo of play.
- If a winger is under pressure, it is the cierre's job to drop deeper to create a safe passing option.
- When playing as a pivot, players should stretch the pitch to make it as long as possible.
- Long rotations make it harder for defenders to apply pressure.
- The movement of players should always be connected to the position of the opposition, taking into account where the ball is on court.
- Players should always look to open passing lines.

Progression Ideas:

- Allow the defending team to counter-attack if they win the ball back.
- Play a full game with each team attempting to rotate as a 3-1 with a false pivot at all times.

Links to Football:

- When teams attack, they all attack together. Defenders do not just defend, they are also integral in initiating and orchestrating attacks.
- The role of the middle player of the three in this drill mimics that of a central defensive midfielder.
- Central defensive midfielders must dictate the tempo of a game, playing forward when possible and using a wide range of passes.
- Traditionally in England, central defensive midfielders are 'stoppers'. The modern game, however, sees this position as a 'starter'. In this drill, the cierre starts moves and controls attacks, acting as a 'starter'.
- False 9s need to understand when to stay high and when to rotate back into midfield to receive the ball.
- If the ball is played forward to the number 9, midfield players must support the attack. This can be done by getting set backs or by running beyond the line.

Session: Rotating as a 4-0

- **Recommended Time:** 20 minutes
- **Number of Players:** 9+

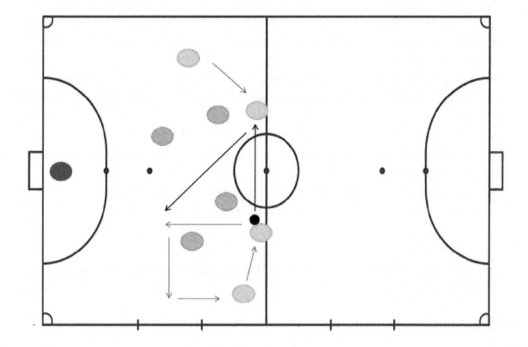

Focus of Session: Passing, movement and finishing.

Objectives: For players to understand the basic movements required to play in a 4-0 system.

Organisation: A defending team of four players – plus a goalkeeper – sets up in any system to defend their own half. The attacking team of four players sets up on the halfway line and has ten chances to score. The goalkeeper begins the practice by throwing the ball to one of the four attacking players positioned on the halfway line. These players rotate as a 4-0 in an attempt to score. Once they have had their ten chances, the teams switch over.

Coaching Factors:

- When rotating as a 4-0, players move the ball laterally. Passes are no longer than ten metres and are made centrally. This is done to engage the first defender.
- Once a player makes a pass they drive forward to a more advanced position on the same side of the court from which they passed the ball.
- The wider player on the same side of the court as the passer then moves more centrally to receive the next pass.
- Once a player has rotated forward, they either receive the ball in an advanced position or rotate back into the line of four and start the rotation again.
- Players should always face forward with their first touch.
- Keeping the ball in central areas will give the player in possession more passing options.
- Dynamic forward runs are needed in order to disrupt defences.
- Change the angle, pace and depth of runs to lose defenders.
- When attacking in the 4-0 system, teams must be patient: the openings will come.
- The ball needs to be moved quickly to disrupt defenders. Always pass the ball with tempo.

Progression Ideas:

- The defending team can counter-attack when they win the ball and score in the opposite goal.
- If the attacking team scores a goal then their set number of chances resets, i.e. if they had ten chances to score then they get another ten.
- When attacking, try and transition from a 4-0 system to a 3-1. This is often done when the opposition's best defender has been disrupted, allowing the weaker defenders to be exploited.

Links to Football:

- When attacking players synchronise their movement patterns, compact defences can be exploited. Pressure can also be released through this synchronisation, allowing teams to play forward more easily.
- Forward movements affect defenders, earning attacking teams both time and space.
- This drill allows players to understand the importance of combination play and choreographed movements resulting from triggers (i.e. lack of

defensive pressure, passing lines being opened).
- When playing as a 4-0, players are often under intense pressure from opponents. This drill encourages players to embrace the pressure and exploit space in behind.
- Translating to midfielders, this drill not only helps players to keep the ball under pressure, but also to play either sideways or forward rather than backwards. In turn, this allows players to face forward in possession in higher areas of the pitch more often.

Chapter 5: Goalkeeping

In modern football the role of the goalkeeper has evolved. No longer is the goalkeeper solely responsible for protecting the goal. Nowadays, the goalkeeper is seen as an extra defender. In turn, the role of pioneers such as Manuel Neuer and Victor Valdes has seen the emergence of 'sweeper keepers' – goalkeepers who are as comfortable with the ball at their feet as they are with the ball in their hands.

This comfort with the ball allows for possession to be circulated through the keeper if a team comes under too much pressure, and also enables a goalkeeper to quickly initiate any attacks. Futsal is a sport where the goalkeeper's involvement is vital to successful attacks. Soft shots into the goalkeeper's hands provide an opportunity for the keeper to start a counter-attack. This can be done through a pinpoint throw, a pass, or even by the goalkeeper travelling with the ball. Furthermore, the concept of powerplaying – where the goalkeeper leaves his goal to play as a fifth outfield player – setting up in the opponent's half – means that the goalkeeper is vital to creating goal-scoring opportunities and that he must be comfortable in possession.

Despite this, goalkeepers still need to be adept at keeping the ball out of their net. Due to the extra speed of a futsal ball, blocking is a key component of successful goalkeeping. Goalkeepers need to adopt different blocking techniques depending on the context. If the goalkeeper does not want to over-commit, they should utilise the 'one-knee block'. This allows the goalkeeper to cover the goal with both the legs and the hands, and also enables goalkeepers to recover quickly should they need to (after their initial save). Whilst blocking, goalkeepers should drop their body towards the floor, keeping their eyes on the ball at all times. If 1v1, the goalkeeper should remain as big as possible, attempting to cover all four corners of the goal whilst delaying the attacker. The longer the goalkeeper delays the attacker, the greater the chance of defenders recovering.

Alternatively, a goalkeeper can use a two-knee block. In this technique, they drop both knees to slide and block the ball. Committing themselves to the ground in this manner means that recovery for a further save takes longer. With this technique, as with one-knee blocks, it is important for the goalkeeper not to allow too much space between their legs and the floor, otherwise an attacker will be able to score along the ground. The keeper's head should be kept forward; this will keep his bodyweight forward and give the keeper momentum into the attacker. Most importantly, the timing of the block is vital – if the goalkeeper goes down too early it allows his opponent time to scoop the ball over him, too late and the ball can be shot along the ground.

Ultimately, goalkeepers need to make themselves as big as possible and have quick reactions to keep the ball out of their net. They play a pivotal role in any team, with their importance elevated in the small-sided game. As such, goalkeepers need to train well. The techniques that they learn can then be transferred successfully to eleven-a-side games.

Session: Defending 1v1 Situations 1

- **Recommended Time:** 20 minutes
- **Number of Players:** 6+

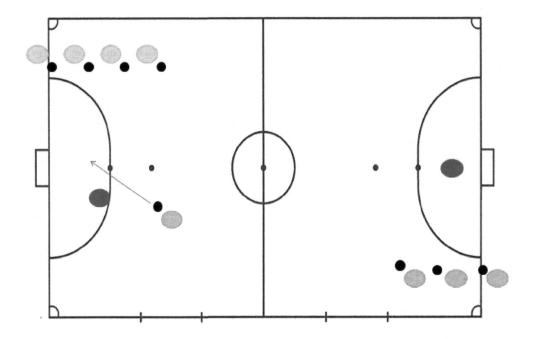

Focus of Session: Position, body shape, blocking and shot-stopping.

Objectives: To develop the goalkeeper's technique in dealing with 1v1 situations when the attacker is through on goal.

Organisation: Players are split evenly into two teams and each given a ball. They then line up in the corner on their own touchline. The blues begin the practice, with the first player dribbling at the opponent's goalkeeper. To score a goal, the player must dribble around the goalkeeper before putting the ball in the net. Once the first 1v1 situation has come to a conclusion – a goal, a save, or the ball going out of play – the first green player attacks. When this attack concludes, the second player on the blue team attacks. The practice carries on in this manner.

Coaching Factors:

- The goalkeeper should focus on his starting position in relation to the ball, always being on the front foot.
- When the opponent attacks the goal, the goalkeeper needs to assess whether to advance or stay and defend the goal.
- The goalkeeper's decision puts the onus on the attacker.
- To force the attacker wide, the goalkeeper should stay on his feet for as long as possible.
- Assess the goalkeeper's technique for blocking.

Progression Ideas:

- Attackers are able to score from anywhere, rather than having to dribble around the goalkeeper.
- Limit the amount of time an attacker has to score.
- Once an attacker has completed their attack, they immediately become a recovering defender and assist the goalkeeper in stopping their opponent from scoring. The exercise continues for two minutes with the coach keeping score between the two teams.

Links to Football:

- Goalkeepers need spatial awareness in both futsal and football for a number of scenarios, such as saving, blocking, and commanding their areas.
- This exercise works on spatial awareness, and also improves decision-making by encouraging the goalkeeper to use the appropriate technique at the right time.
- In this exercise, the goalkeeper has to stay as big as possible for as long as possible to force the attacker away from danger.
- When dealing with 1v1 attacks, goalkeepers often have to save the ball with their feet or block.

Session: Defending 1v1 Situations 2

- **Recommended Time:** 20 minutes
- **Number of Players:** 10+

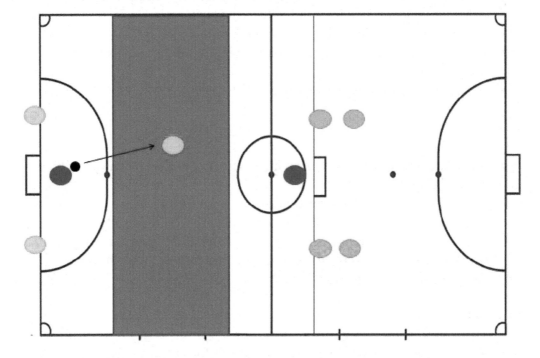

Focus of Session: Position, body shape, blocking and shot-stopping.

Objectives: To develop the goalkeeper's ability to deal with 1v1 situations.

Organisation: The practice is begun by the green team's goalkeeper throwing the ball to a green in the central zone. Attacking players must receive the ball in this zone. The green player attacks the opposition goalkeeper unopposed. The attacking player may only score a goal once he is within seven metres of the goalkeeper. Once he has attacked, the blue's goalkeeper throws the ball to a blue in the central zone, who attacks the opponent's goalkeeper.

Coaching Factors:

- The goalkeeper needs to decide whether to advance or stay and defend the goal. This depends upon any pressure on the ball and where the ball is on the court.
- Communication is vital.
- The defender and goalkeeper need to communicate so that one of them engages the ball and the other defends the goal and attempts to cut out passing lines to the far post.
- Work on blocking techniques – use the appropriate technique for the situation.
- Goalkeepers should not turn their head when blocking. Eyes must be kept on the ball at all times.

Progression Ideas:

- Attackers only have 5 seconds to score.
- Attackers are opposed. Once they have attacked, they become the defender.
- An extra attacker joins in, creating a 2v1 overload for the attacking team. The player that has the final touch in an attack becomes the defender in the next attack, with the other player stepping out. These attacks are done alternately between teams so that each player rotates regularly between attacking and defending.

Links to Football:

- This exercise requires goalkeepers to make good decisions in game situations.
- When dealing with 1v1 attacks, goalkeepers often have to save the ball with their feet or block.
- Communication with defenders is vitally important in the final progression of this practice. The goalkeeper needs to know when, what, and how to communicate at any given moment. This is equally important in football.

Session: Defending 1v1 Situations 3

- **Recommended Time:** 20 minutes
- **Number of Players:** 10

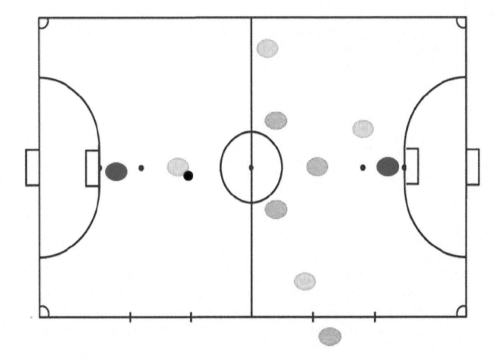

Focus of Session: Position, body shape, blocking and shot-stopping.

Objectives: To develop the goalkeeper's ability to deal with 1v1 scenarios in a game situation.

Organisation: A conditioned game is played between two teams with a goal moved to the edge of the D at both ends. When a team loses possession, one of their players must drop out of the court to create an overload for the attacking team. Players take it in turns to leave the court.

Coaching Factors:

- Work on the goalkeeper's position in relation to the ball. This includes whether to advance or stay and protect the goal.
- In a 1v1 situation, the goalkeeper should make himself as big as possible for as long as possible.
- Assess the goalkeeper's technique for blocking.
- Communication is key between the goalkeeper and his teammates.

Progression Ideas:

- Two players drop out when their team loses possession, creating a greater overload.
- Defending teams must press high up the court. This will leave more space in behind, increasing the likelihood of the goalkeeper having to defend 1v1.

Links to Football:

- The goalkeeper must communicate with his teammates and work together with them.
- With effective positioning, the goalkeeper can delay attackers and usher them away from dangerous areas.
- This exercise mimics defending a counter-attack in football. The team must defend when outnumbered.
- If the goalkeeper defends his goal well, he can initiate counter-attacks for his own team.

Session: Control, Passing and Distribution 1

- **Recommended Time:** 20 minutes
- **Number of Players:** 6+

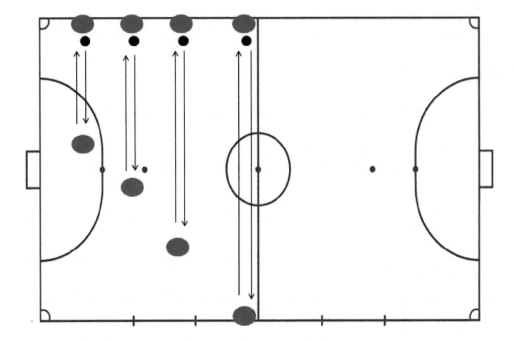

Focus of Session: Passing and control.

Objectives: To encourage the goalkeeper to use different parts of his body to control the ball, and then pass or throw the ball over short, medium and long distances using a variety of techniques.

Organisation: The goalkeepers work in pairs across the court, standing a determined distance apart. The two goalkeepers pass a ball between each other, making sure there is enough weight on the ball to cover the desired distance.

Coaching Factors:

- The weight of the pass/throw has to be firm enough to cover the desired distance, but not so firm that the receiver cannot control the ball.
- Work on the trajectory of the pass/throw – the flatter the better, but too flat and opponents may be able to intercept the ball.
- Speed of pass/throw.
- Accuracy of pass/throw.
- Passes/throws should be aimed at the receiver's 'safe side'.
- Positional sense – analyse the position of both the deliverer and the receiver.

Progression Ideas:

- The two goalkeepers stand 6-8m apart and pass the ball to each other using the instep, controlling the ball with the sole of their foot.
- The two goalkeepers stand 10-12m apart and drive the ball to each other using the top of their foot, controlling the ball with the sole.
- The two goalkeepers stand 15-18m apart and scoop the ball to each other using the front of the foot, controlling the ball with different parts of the body (foot, thigh, chest, head, etc).
- The two goalkeepers stand 18-20m apart. The goalkeeper with the ball dribbles to the middle, stops the ball with the sole of their foot, and then passes the ball using either the sole or the inside of their foot.

Links to Football:

- In the modern game, goalkeepers are expected to act as an extra defender, being confident on the ball and able to play out from the back.
- This exercise works on the competence of goalkeepers with the ball at their feet.
- Goalkeepers need to be able to control the ball with all parts of their body. They need to do this to be able to change the direction of the attack and keep the ball secure.
- Control needs to be instant with a quick decision made. This is because attackers will close the goalkeeper down quickly, limiting any time on the ball.
- Once a keeper has the ball under control, they are able to start an attack, or switch the play to change the direction of an attack.
- This can be done with a short pass. Long passes can also be used to clear the ball or find players at distance.

- If a keeper comes to claim a cross or catches the ball, he can initiate a quick counter-attack by throwing the ball.
- This exercise teaches different throwing techniques, which can be used depending on where opponents and teammates are situated.

Session: Control, Passing and Distribution 2

- **Recommended Time:** 20 minutes
- **Number of Players:** 10+

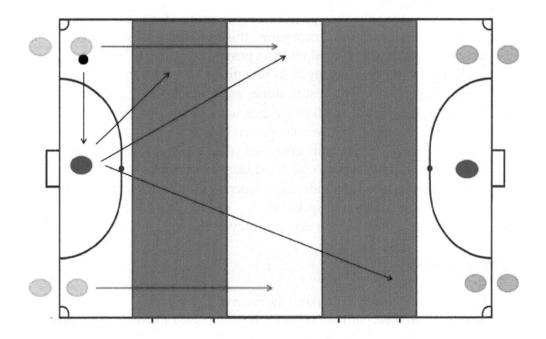

Focus of Session: Passing and control.

Objectives: For the goalkeeper to control the ball and distribute it successfully over a variety of distances.

Organisation: The green team begin the exercise by playing the ball into their goalkeeper. The first green pair then make forward runs. The goalkeeper then distributes the ball – with either his feet or hands – to one of the players making the forward run. This player must receive the ball in one of the three zones marked out. The goalkeeper needs to decide the appropriate technique depending upon the distance the ball must travel and the position on the court of the receiver. The player receiving the ball must then play it into the blue player directly in front of them. The exercise is then repeated with the other goalkeeper and the pair of blues.

Coaching Factors:

- Assess the angle and distance of the goalkeeper's support position.
- The goalkeeper needs to communicate where he wants the ball.
- The goalkeeper needs to be composed when receiving the ball and able to play the ball using both feet.
- Goalkeepers are only allowed to be in possession of the ball for four seconds in their own half. Incorporate this into the practice. Whilst striving to remain composed when in possession of the ball, the goalkeeper must be encouraged to act quickly and efficiently.
- Select the receiver in the best position, assessing his body position.
- Assess the technique a goalkeeper uses when passing to feet or into space – sole roll, side foot, drill, wedge, driven ball, scoop.
- Assess the technique a goalkeeper uses when throwing to feet or into space – underarm, javelin, 'chuck', sidearm, overarm.
- The goalkeeper needs to understand when to play the ball to the receiver's feet and when to play into space.
- Work on the timing, weight and accuracy of the pass.

Progression Ideas:

- Develop the practice by making the receiving player pass the ball diagonally to their partner once they have received the ball. This player then passes it to the next pair.
- Once a player receives the ball, he can shoot at the opposite goalkeeper.

Links to Football:

- If a player has space to drive into, the keeper should throw the ball in front of him. If he is under pressure, however, the ball should be thrown to the player's 'safe side'.
- When counter-attacking, players make dynamic runs forward to receive the ball without having to break their stride. Poor passes/throws may cause counter-attacks to break down.
- Goalkeepers must be able to distribute effectively to a number of different areas on the pitch.

Session: Control, Passing and Distribution 3

- **Recommended Time:** 20 minutes
- **Number of Players:** 12

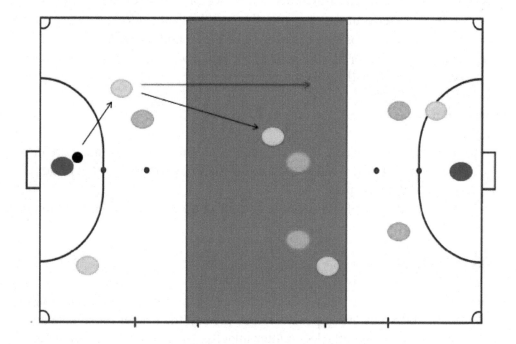

Focus of Session: Passing.

Objectives: For the goalkeeper to distribute the ball successfully in a game situation.

Organisation: The full court is split into thirds. Teams organise themselves into a 1-2-2-1 formation. To begin with, the goalkeepers can only distribute the ball into their own defensive thirds. Once a player receives the ball from the goalkeeper they can either run the ball into the next third or pass it in. One of the two players can then join in with the two players in the middle third to create a 3v2 overload. Play then continues with the team in possession attempting to get into the attacking third, where a maximum of two players can join the lone attacker already in that third in an attempt to score. Defenders must stick to their areas.

Coaching Factors:

- Communication is needed between the goalkeeper and defenders.
- Work on the weight, trajectory, speed, and accuracy of the pass/throw.
- If the receiver is under pressure, throw to his 'safe side'.
- Understand the position of both the deliverer and receiver.
- Once a goalkeeper has distributed the ball, they must offer a support position so the ball can be recycled.

Progression Ideas:

- An extra player is added to the attacking team's middle zone to create a 3v2 overload. The goalkeeper can now only distribute into the middle third to begin the play.
- Players can now play anywhere and the goalkeeper can distribute into any of the thirds.

Links to Football:

- Distribution of the ball by the goalkeeper is of utmost importance for the team. Once they are in possession of the ball the keeper must have an awareness to start attacks/counter-attacks. The ball must be distributed with good technique and accuracy to enable the team to keep possession of the ball in an attempt to score against the opponent.
- The goalkeeper must be able to distribute the ball with the hand in the form of throwing in a variety of ways, depending on what type of technique is called for, during different stages of the game.
- Similar to a variety of throwing techniques, the goalkeeper needs to be capable of distributing the ball with his feet in a number of different ways.
- All decisions regarding distribution must be based upon the position of opponents and teammates, and is dependent upon pressure.
- Both visual and verbal communication plays a huge part in the process.

Chapter 6: Fitness

At first glance, the fact that futsal teams are allowed 14 players in a matchday squad seems a little excessive. There are, of course, only four outfield players playing at any one time. Upon playing the game, however, you can soon see why teams choose to have such numbers in their squads.

Futsal is a dynamic game with no room for passengers. With only four outfield players on the court at any one time, teams must attack together and defend together. Whereas players spend around 70% of a football game engaging in low-intensity activity, such as walking and jogging, futsal is characterised by explosive bursts of acceleration, quick changes of direction and sudden stopping. The ball moves quicker so players must also move quicker.

Teams are allowed rolling substitutions. This means that players can maintain a high intensity when on court and then come off to recover when tired. Much of futsal tests a player's anaerobic energy system. They must be able to constantly repeat high intensity actions during a game. Failure to do so can have a negative impact on the team.

Working at such high intensity is beneficial for when a player transfers from the futsal court to the football pitch. Players will find that they are able to delay the onset of fatigue, that they can continue to work at a high intensity without any detriment to their technical ability, and that they can go faster for further and longer. For players such as full backs, who, in the modern game, must work up and down the pitch at a high intensity for the full 90 minutes, this is essential.

It should be noted that all of the exercises shown in the previous chapters can be modified so that they are focused on fitness. For example, when playing a game, a coach may introduce the rule that if a player loses possession, he must run to the opponent's goal and touch the crossbar before being allowed to re-enter the game.

The following exercises, however, are aimed solely at improving elements of fitness in players. Their main purposes can be split into three sections: anaerobic endurance, aerobic endurance, and acceleration-deceleration. As with previous exercises, the focus should be on player enjoyment. The use of balls and game-realistic scenarios – such as 1v1 actions – is therefore encouraged.

Session: Aerobic Endurance

- **Time:** 40 minutes (4 sets of 8 minutes with 2 minutes rest in between sets)

- **Number of players:** 12+

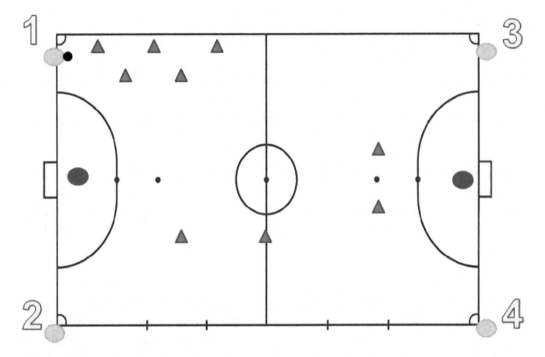

Focus of Session: Conditioning.

Objectives: To improve players' aerobic endurance.

Organisation: Players are split evenly between the four corners. Each corner has a different exercise. One player from each corner starts their exercise at the same time. Whilst they are completing this exercise, the other players at the corner perform an exercise chosen by the coach. This may be sit-ups, press-ups or burpees, for example.

At Corner One, cones are laid out diagonally at five-metre intervals. Players must dribble in and out of these cones as quickly as possible. Just before the halfway line they have to sprint for ten metres before shooting at the goal from ten metres out. After this shot they turn towards Corner Two. They then sprint forward to the cone marked out over the halfway line, backpedal to the halfway line, and then jog to Corner Two whilst recovering.

Players at Corner Two sprint the length of the court and then walk to recover and get to Corner Three.

At Corner Three, players sprint diagonally for ten metres to collect a ball. They then travel at pace at the goal ahead to go 1v1 against the goalkeeper. Once this action is over, the player will jog around the court to Corner Four. Here they will perform the exercise that the coach has allocated, for example, a 30-second plank.

Coaching Factors:

- Sprints and actions with the ball must be at 100%.
- The recovery jog can be as slow as needed to allow a proper recovery to perform the next actions at maximum intensity.
- Assess the speed at which players are able to change direction.

Progression Ideas:

- Exercises at the corners can be eliminated or modified for each set.
- Increase either the number of sets or the duration of each set.
- All exercises must be performed with a ball. This includes any recovery jogs.
- To progress this further, players must use their weak foot when dribbling with the ball.

Links to Football:

- Football is an intermittent sport. A player's average heart rate during a game is around 85% of their maximal value.
- Running, at any intensity, for 90 minutes, requires a high level of stamina.
- In a 90-minute football match, players will run around 10-13km.
- Working on these drills will improve a player's aerobic capacity, allowing them to play to the best of their ability for longer.
- This is vital, as players must be able to perform technical skills such as dribbling at a high intensity even when tired.

Session: Anaerobic Endurance

- **Time:** 15 minutes (3 sets of 4 minutes with 1 minute of rest in between)
- **Number of players:** 12+

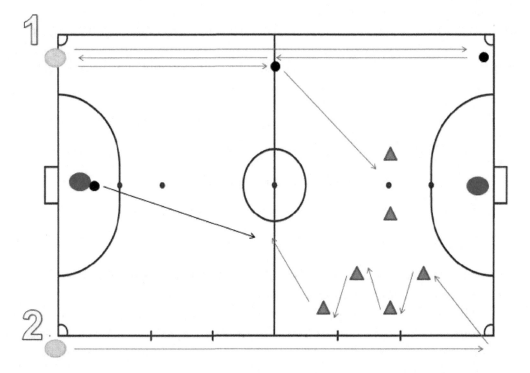

Focus of Session: Conditioning.

Objectives: To improve players' anaerobic endurance through actions specific to futsal.

Organisation: Players are split evenly between the two corners with one goalkeeper in each goal.

From Corner One, players sprint the length of the court. Once they get to the opposite corner they collect a ball and dribble up to the halfway line. Here they stop the ball on the line, sprint back to their start point, turn back once again and collect the ball for a second time. They then dribble until they are ten metres from goal and take a shot.

At Corner Two, a player sprints the length of the court. Once he gets to the opposite corner he turns and sprints in and out of the four diagonal cones. As

112

soon as he reaches the halfway line he receives a ball from the goalkeeper, against whom he then performs a 1v1. Once this action is complete, the player joins Corner One.

Players not exercising are resting whilst waiting at the corner.

Coaching Factors:

- Sprints and actions with the ball must be done at 100%.
- Work on arm movement, body positioning and effective movement when changing direction.
- In the first few yards, players should keep their body low and take big strong strides to accelerate.
- Technical details with the ball should not suffer as a result of fatigue.

Progression Ideas:

- Movements with more changes of direction can be included.
- Exercises can be included at the corner before starting the exercise.
- All sprints must be performed with the ball.
- Add technical details to each station. For example, players at Corner Two must shoot into the goal once they reach the opposite corner.

Links to Football:

- The capacity to repeat high-intensity movements within a short period of time is vital in both football and futsal.
- The frequency of high-intensity running undertaken in matches has been shown to be what separates top level players from those at a lower level.
- Performing technical skills at a high level is hard when fatigued. This exercise encourages players to value the ball when they are tired.
- A position such as full back requires players to recover quickly from maximal sprints. If a full back overlaps and the attack breaks down, he must sprint back quickly to recover.

Session: Anaerobic Endurance & General Conditioning

- **Time:** 15 mins (3 sets of 30 seconds at each station with 1 minute of rest in between stations)
- **Number of Players:** 18+

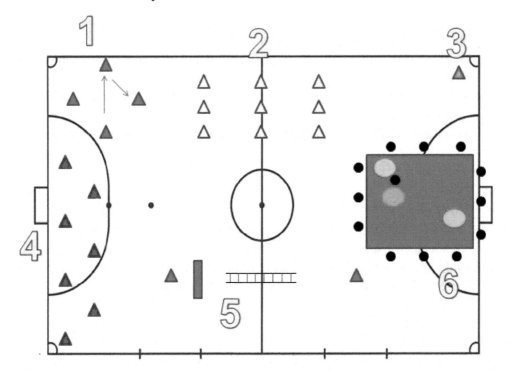

Focus of Session: Conditioning.

Objectives: To improve anaerobic endurance and the general condition of the players through actions specific to futsal.

Organisation: Players are split evenly between the six stations. There must be three players at each station.

At each station, players work at maximum intensity for 30 seconds. When not working, they are resting. Upon completing each station, players move to the next station. The stations compromise the following:

Station 1: Players sprint forward from the start-point and then backpedal to the cone on the right. They then return to the start-point and repeat the action, this time backpedalling to the left cone.

Station 2: At maximum speed, players must dribble around the three cones in each line.

Station 3: 30 seconds of lunges, push-ups and sit-ups. Players work continuously throughout the 90 seconds.

Station 4: Players dribble in and out of all the cones with the ball. One player works at a time.

Station 5: Players jump over the hurdle with both feet and then accelerate through the agility ladder. The coach dictates how they go through the ladder (in and out, hopscotch, one foot in each, etc.).

Station 6: In a small 5x5m area, players play in 2v1 possession drill. Balls must be set-up around the outside to keep the intensity high during each set of 30 seconds. At the end of each 30-second period, the defender changes. If the defender gets possession of the ball they must keep it for as long as possible.

Coaching Factors:

- Sprints and actions with the ball must be at 100% during the 30 seconds of work.
- Assess the technique of sprinting and jumping.
- Players should be in full control of the ball whilst sprinting.
- Assess acceleration and deceleration.

Progression Ideas:

- Different stations can be included, focusing on the aspects the coach feels his players need to improve (i.e. a station focusing on passing).
- Reduce the recovery period between stations.
- Repeat the whole circuit a set amount of times.
- When working with the ball, players must use their weak foot.
- Add a competitive edge to the session. Make certain stations competitive by having two players going at once, racing against each other.

Links to Football:

- Players need speed and speed endurance to continue playing at their maximum capacity throughout the 90 minutes.
- Most players will perform more than 150 intense actions during a game. This requires a high turnover of anaerobic energy, as well as utilisation of creatine phosphate.
- Plyomteric exercises increase leg power. This helps players gain the edge when completing their intense actions. Greater power will help players jump higher to win headers and accelerate ahead of their opponent.

Session: Acceleration-Deceleration

- **Time:** 20 minutes
- **Number of players:** 10+

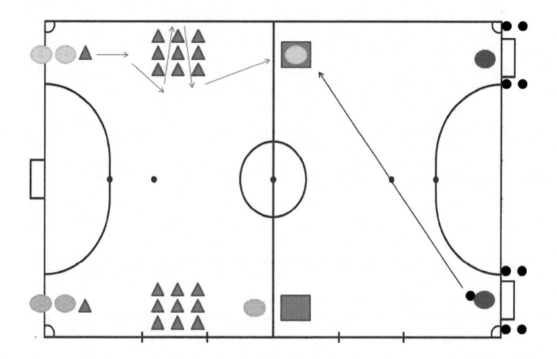

Focus of Session: Speed (acceleration/deceleration).

Objectives: To improve the acceleration-deceleration of the players through a futsal-based drill.

Organisation: Players are split evenly between two teams. They then line up behind their allocated cone, facing a player on the opposing team.

Seven metres in front of their start-point there are three rows of three cones. Just over the halfway line there is a 1x1m square. On the opposite side of the court there are two goals, both placed in the corners.

The coach begins the practice by shouting 'go'. On this command, the player at the front of the line races his opponent, sprinting in and out of the cones at maximal speed. Once through, players accelerate into the square. The first player to sit down in their square becomes the attacker, and receives a ball from the goalkeeper straight ahead of him. The player who sits down second will be the defender. The attacker will then attack the opposite goal (diagonal to him). This will give time for the defender to recover.

Coaching Factors:

- Make sure all actions are done at maximal speed.
- Players should maintain a low centre of gravity to aid acceleration/deceleration.
- The first stride when accelerating should be big and powerful. This should set the tone for a high-intensity burst forward.
- Push off powerfully from the ground with each step.
- Assess technique. Look at the position of the player's arms and legs. Arms should be pumped with the elbow at 90 degrees.
- On contact with the ground, the toes should provide the force to push off with the heel staying off the ground.
- Work on players having stiffness in their ankles, pulling toes to shin. Knees drive through.
- Players should change direction quickly and efficiently.
- Look at the reaction times of the players and how this affects their initial acceleration.
- Work on recovery runs for the defender.
- Make sure the attacking player is as positive as possible. They should punish the defender.

Progression Ideas:

- Alter the position of the cones to include different movements.
- Players begin the practice sitting down.
- Increase the competitiveness by awarding each team a point for every goal they score.
- Once players have completed their action, rather than returning to their team's queue, they stay next to the goals to create an overload in the next attack. Players who attack can then use these players to get set-backs.

Links to Football:

- Both football and futsal are dynamic sports which require a great number of changes in speeds and directions.
- Numerous decisive match actions are dictated by players' acceleration. Players must get to the ball before their opponent.

- This is especially vital in the opponent's penalty area. A quick acceleration away from a defender can lead to a shot at goal, or even to being brought down by a late challenge for a penalty kick.
- Increases in a player's acceleration will also lead to increases in their explosive power. This aids other parts of their game, such as jumping to compete for headers.

Chapter 7: Final Thoughts

Futsal is not necessarily the answer to England's 11-a-side problems. However, if incorporated into the development of players, the technical and tactical benefits will be enormous. There is certainly a strong argument for its inclusion within the English football season. Currently, the bulk of the season is played in bad weather. Players can go months without playing a competitive game. If they do manage to play, they are often subjected to poor conditions and near-unplayable pitches. Encouraging players to pass the ball along the floor is certainly complicated when they are met by a mudbath with a goal at either end. In such circumstances, why would players pass the ball short? And how could they possibly attempt to dribble and create? No, in such circumstances the long punt forward is often the most effective option.

This limits development. In such situations, the physical qualities outweigh the technical qualities. Enjoyment also comes into the equation. In poor conditions players often don't want to be there, referees often don't want to be there, and parents often don't want to be there. If a player doesn't enjoy playing then development will be limited. It is important to improve players technically, tactically, socially and psychologically. To do this, players must be in a positive mental state, motivated and willing to learn.

Futsal is a sport that allows players to express themselves. Games are not affected by the weather. The surface always allows players to pass the ball and dribble against their opponents. The technical outweighs the physical.

In an elite football game, the ball is in play for an average of 53 minutes. In the grassroots game, where pitches are not enclosed, this time is even less. In futsal, however, the ball is in play for 40 minutes every game. With five people making up a team, players get many more touches of the ball when playing futsal. The number of critical moments – 1v1s, shots, interchanges, combinations – are increased for each player in comparison to the 11-a-side game. Inevitably, this impacts upon decision-making. When the speed of the game is also considered, it can be concluded that players need to make good decisions regularly when under pressure in tight areas. It is, therefore, no surprise that continental players, who have been influenced by futsal since an early age, tend to make better decisions in the 11-a-side game.

Futsal is not 5-a-side. It is a highly tactical sport. Players have to adapt to a number of different systems and positions throughout a game. Traditionally, futsal has been known for its technical benefits. People look at the sport and see it as a means of showing off skills, dribbling, and improving individual ability. When looked at closely, however, it can be seen that futsal is a team sport which is also highly tactical. Players learn how to rotate and interchange, to play in a number of different positions, to attack as a unit, defend as a unit, transition between attack and defence, and to press. All of these decisions are dictated by triggers, such as the position of players on the pitch. These factors are all essential in the 11-a-side game.

The need for players to play in all positions has enormous benefits for the 11-a-side game. In the modern game, footballers must be comfortable in a number of positions. Attackers must be able to defend, defenders must be able to attack, and players must all be confident in possession of the ball whilst under pressure. Too often, in junior football, the worst players at the age of eight are shepherded into defence, the most physically developed players are put into midfield positions, and the best players are the goal scorers. If players remain in these positions, as they so often do, they become one-dimensional. Futsal creates innovative problem-solvers, just as comfortable in front of their opponent's goal as they are defending their own.

This book offers guidance for you, the coach, on futsal and how it can be used to develop modern footballers. The outlined sessions provide the tools for a player to improve their overall game. However, it should be noted that it is also important for players to take part in unorganised practices. It is your job to guide, not to dictate. Let players find their own solutions to problems. Don't create robotic clones. Take pride in their development. Applaud innovation. Encourage mistakes. Praise players for trying.

Most importantly, make sure that sessions are set up to allow players to enjoy their work. Remember that you need to develop players socially, psychologically, tactically and technically. The framework has been provided. Now, it is over to you. Give futsal a go. You won't regret it, and neither will your players.

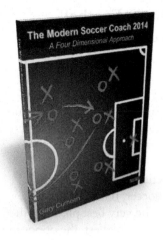

The Modern Soccer Coach by Gary Curneen

Aimed at Soccer coaches of all levels and with players of all ages and abilities The Modern Soccer Coach 2014 identifies the areas that must be targeted by coaches who want to maximize a team's potential – the Technical, Tactical, Physical, and Mental sides to the game. See how the game has changed and what areas determine success in the game today. Learn what sets coaches like Mourinho, Klopp, Rodgers, and Guardiola apart from the rest. Philosophies and training methods from the most forward thinking coaches in the game today are presented, along with guidelines on creating a modern environment for readers' teams. This book is not about old school methodologies – it is about creating a culture of excellence that gets the very best from players. Contains more than 30 illustrated exercises that focus on tactical, technical, mental, and physical elements of the game.

Jose Mourinho: The Rise of the Translator by Ciaran Kelly

From growing up in a Portugal emerging from dictatorship, and struggling to live up to his father's legacy as an international goalkeeper, the book details José Mourinho's extraordinary journey: the trophies, tragedies and, of course, the fall-outs. Starting out as a translator for the late Sir Bobby Robson, Mourinho has come to define a new breed of manager, with his unrivalled use of psychology, exhaustive research, and man management providing ample compensation for an unremarkable playing career. Mourinho has gone on to become one of the greatest managers of all-time. From Porto to Chelsea, and Inter to Real Madrid – the Mourinho story is as intriguing as the man himself. Now, a new challenge awaits at Stamford Bridge. Covering the Mourinho story to October 2013 and featuring numerous exclusive interviews with figures not synonymous with the traditional Mourinho narrative.

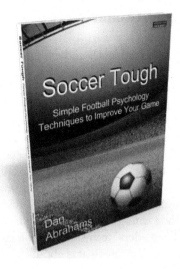

Soccer Tough: Simple Football Psychology Techniques to Improve Your Game by Dan Abrahams

"Take a minute to slip into the mind of one of the world's greatest soccer players and imagine a stadium around you. Picture a performance under the lights and mentally play the perfect game."

Technique, speed and tactical execution are crucial components of winning soccer, but it is mental toughness that marks out the very best players – the ability to play when pressure is highest, the opposition is strongest, and fear is greatest. Top players and coaches understand the importance of sport psychology in soccer but how do you actually train your mind to become the best player you can be? Soccer Tough demystifies this crucial side of the game and offers practical techniques that will enable soccer players of all abilities to actively develop focus, energy, and confidence. Soccer Tough will help banish the fear, mistakes, and mental limits that holds players back.

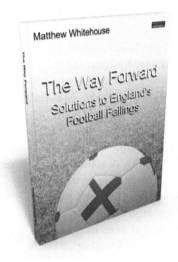

The Way Forward: Solutions to England's Football Failings
by Matthew Whitehouse

English football is in a state of crisis. It has been almost 50 years since England made the final of a major championship and the national sides, at all levels, continue to disappoint and underperform. Yet no-one appears to know how to improve the situation. In his acclaimed book, The Way Forward, football coach Matthew Whitehouse examines the causes of English football's decline and offers a number of areas where change and improvement need to be implemented immediately. With a keen focus and passion for youth development and improved coaching he explains that no single fix can overcome current difficulties and that a multi-pronged strategy is needed. If we wish to improve the standards of players in England then we must address the issues in schools, the grassroots, and academies, as well as looking at the constraints of the Premier League and English FA.

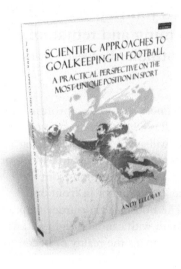

Scientific Approaches to Goalkeeping in Football: A practical perspective on the most unique position in sport
by Andy Elleray

Do you coach goalkeepers and want to help them realise their fullest potential? Are you a goalkeeper looking to reach the top of your game? Then search no further and dive into this dedicated goalkeeping resource. Written by goalkeeping guru Andy Elleray this book offers a fresh and innovative approach to goalkeeping in football. With a particular emphasis on the development of young goalkeepers, it sheds light on training, player development, match performances, and player analysis. Utilising his own experiences Andy shows the reader various approaches, systems and exercises that will enable goalkeepers to train effectively and appropriately to bring out the very best in them.

The Modern Soccer Coach: Position-Specific Training by Gary Curneen

Aimed at football coaches of all levels, and players of all ages and abilities, The Modern Soccer Coach: Position-Specific Training seeks to identify, develop, and enhance the skills and functions of the modern soccer player whatever their position and role on the pitch.

This book offers unique insight into how to develop an elite program that can both improve players and win games. Filled with practical no-nonsense explanations, focused player drills, and more than 40 illustrated soccer templates, this book will help you – the modern coach - to create a coaching environment that will take your players to the next level.

The Footballer's Journey: real-world advice on becoming and remaining a professional footballer by Dean Caslake and Guy Branston

Many youngsters dream of becoming a professional footballer. But football is a highly competitive world where only a handful will succeed. Many aspiring soccer players don't know exactly what to expect, or what is required, to make the transition from the amateur world to the 'bright lights' in front of thousands of fans. The Footballer's Journey maps out the footballer's path with candid insight and no-nonsense advice. It examines the reality of becoming a footballer including the odds of 'making it', how academies really work, the importance of attitude and mindset, and even the value of having a backup plan if things don't quite work out.

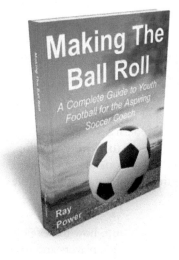

Making The Ball Roll: A Complete Guide to Youth Football for the Aspiring Soccer Coach by Ray Power

Making the Ball Roll is the ultimate complete guide to coaching youth soccer.

This focused and easy-to-understand book details training practices and tactics, and goes on to show you how to help young players achieve peak performance through tactical preparation, communication, psychology, and age-specific considerations. Each chapter covers, in detail, a separate aspect of coaching to give you, the football coach, a broad understanding of youth soccer development. Each topic is brought to life by the stories of real coaches working with real players. Never before has such a comprehensive guide to coaching soccer been found in the one place. If you are a new coach, or just trying to improve your work with players - and looking to invest in your future - this is a must-read book!

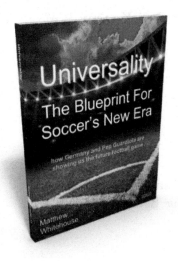

Universality | The Blueprint for Soccer's New Era: How Germany and Pep Guardiola are showing us the Future Football Game by Matthew Whitehouse

The game of soccer is constantly in flux; new ideas, philosophies and tactics mould the present and shape the future. In this book, Matthew Whitehouse – acclaimed author of The Way Forward: Solutions to England's Football Failings - looks in-depth at the past decade of the game, taking the reader on a journey into football's evolution. Examining the key changes that have occurred since the turn of the century, right up to the present, the book looks at the evolution of tactics, coaching, and position-specific play. They have led us to this moment: to the rise of universality. Universality | The Blueprint For Soccer's New Era is a voyage into football, as well as a lesson for coaches, players and fans who seek to know and anticipate where the game of the future is heading.

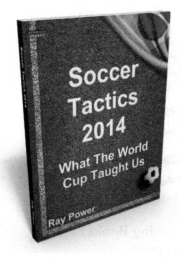

Soccer Tactics 2014: What The World Cup Taught Us by Ray Power

World Cups throw up unique tactical variations. Countries and football cultures from around the globe converge, in one place, to battle it out for world soccer supremacy. The 2014 World Cup in Brazil was no different, arguably throwing up tactical differences like never seen at a competition in modern times. Contests are not just won by strong work ethics and technical brilliance, but by tactical discipline, fluidity, effective strategies, and (even) unique national traits. Soccer Tactics 2014 analyses the intricacies of modern international systems, through the lens of matches in Brazil. Covering formations, game plans, key playing positions, and individuals who bring football tactics to life - the book offers analysis and insights for soccer coaches, football players, and fans the world over. The book sheds light on where football tactics currently stand… and where they are going. Includes analysis of group matches, knock out stages, and the final.

Other Recent Books from Bennion Kearny

Tipping The Balance: The Mental Skills Handbook For Athletes
by Dr Martin Turner & Dr Jamie Barker

The 7 Master Moves of Success
by Jag Shoker

**Paul Webb Academy: Strength Training Books
for Footballers and Goalkeepers**

Learn More about our Books at:

www.BennionKearny.com/Soccer

Lightning Source UK Ltd.
Milton Keynes UK
UKOW07f2111090317
296244UK00004B/18/P

9 781909 125926